*Explora____
& Encounters*

TONY D. TRIGGS

04359

This book is dedicated to the memory of the victims

ACKNOWLEDGEMENTS

The author and publishers would like to thank the following for permission to reproduce photographs and other material:

Neg. No. 329247. Courtesy of the Department of Library Services, American Museum of Natural History	cover; 26
The Trustees of the British Museum	cover; 15; 16; 18; 20-21; 22-23; 24; 25; 27; 31; 32; 34-35; 39; 40
C. M. Dixon Colour Photo Library	31; 37; 41
Mary Evans Picture Library	cover; 10; 26
Michael Holford	6; 8-9; 11; 20; 36; 41
Natural History Photographic Agency	12 (Ivan Polunin); 13 (G. I. Bernard); 14 (Stephen Dalton and Carl Switak); 18 (Philippa Scott); 44 (Douglas Dickens)
National Maritime Museum, London	5
Ronald Sheridan/Ancient Art and Architecture Collection	cover; title page; 4; 5; 25; 28-29; 33; 41; 46-47
The Board of Trustees of the Royal Armouries	46-47
Royal Geographical Society	7
Wellcome Institute Library, London	cover; 42; 43

The publishers have made every effort to contact copyright holders but this has not always been possible. If any have been overlooked we will be pleased to make any necessary arrangements.

First published 1992 by Folens Limited, Dunstable and Dublin.
Folens Limited, Albert House, Apex Business Centre, Boscombe Road, Dunstable LU5 4RL, England.

ISBN 1 85276110-5

Cover Design: Hybert Design & Type.
Illustrator: Peter Dennis of Linda Rogers Associates.

Printed in Singapore by Craft Print.

CONTENTS

One day Europe will no longer be the end of the earth; a sailor will discover a new world.

Christopher Columbus' ship, "Santa Maria".

1. Sailing West

It was the summer of 1492, and the streets of a little Spanish port were unusually busy. A Genoese sea captain called Christopher Columbus was preparing 3 ships for a dangerous journey. There were carpenters finishing off the ships, merchants bringing food, candles and other supplies and 100 sailors shouting noisily. Led by Columbus, they were planning to sail westwards across the stormy Atlantic Ocean.

No one knew what they would find, for the ocean had not been properly explored. Some people thought the earth was flat and that the ships and men would probably disappear over a huge waterfall at its edge.

An astrolabe used for showing the positions of the Sun and stars.

The shape of the earth was a very important question. Only land to the east of Europe had been explored. Spices and other goods from Asia had to be brought to Spain by a long and difficult route. Spices, grown in islands known as the Indies, were shipped to the Asian mainland and then carried overland to the west coast of India. From here they were shipped to Egypt, and on to Spain (and the rest of western Europe) by sea or land.

Christopher Columbus, 1451-1506.

We now know the world is round.

Merchants who brought the spices from the east faced many dangers. They were sometimes killed by disease or bandits, or lost in storms at sea. These difficulties meant spices were very expensive.

Nowadays, we can do without spice, but in those days it was very important. Farmers knew that in winter there would not be enough grass to feed their cattle, sheep and pigs, so they killed a lot of them in the autumn. People preserved the meat with salt or spice, for eating during the winter.

? The need for spice

Read the information given on spice on this page.

1. Why was spice more important in Columbus' time than it is today?
2. Discuss how life would be changed if we had to use spice in the same way today.

A   *A map of the world from 1486.*

Columbus thought that the earth was round like a ball. If this was true, there had to be two different ways to go round it. Merchants from Spain were heading east to get to the Indies, but what if they went the other way? Columbus believed that if they did this they would get to the Indies by an easier route. He wanted to be the first to find it and he was willing to risk his life at sea in order to do so.

Columbus was right about the world being round. But Columbus was also wrong about something. He did not know that North, Central and South America blocked his sea route to the Indies. When he made his voyage he landed on islands off the coast of Central America. He thought he had reached the Indies and he never found out his mistake.

Columbus had found the Americas - a whole New World that people in Europe had never heard of. When they realised the truth they began to call the Indies the East Indies. The islands which Columbus had discovered were known as the West Indies.

Right and wrong

Study maps **A** and **B**.

1. Look at map **A**. Think about when this map was made. Which countries are missing? Why?
2. Map **B** was made after Columbus had discovered the Americas. Compare it with a world map today. Are there any differences? (Look carefully at the shape of South America.)
3. Use map **B** to pick out the journey the spice merchants made in Columbus' time. (Be sure you know where the East Indies are before you begin.)
4. Pretend that you are a merchant living in the 16th century. Use map **B** to plan a new route for bringing spice from the East Indies to Europe.

It is often hard to say why something happened exactly when it did. The timing of Columbus' voyage is linked to something that happened a few months earlier.

For several centuries, most of Spain and Portugal had been ruled by people called Moors who had come from North Africa. During the 15th century, the Spanish and Portuguese gradually pushed the Moors out of their lands. In 1492 they conquered the last Moorish region, Granada. Almost immediately, the King and Queen of Spain, Ferdinand and Isabella, agreed to help Columbus make his voyage.

Why 1492?

Think about what you have read on this page.

1. Why do you think the Spanish King and Queen felt the time was right to help Columbus make his voyage?

B *A world map drawn in 1571.*

TYPVS ORBIS TERRARVM

QVID EI POTEST VIDERI MAGNVM IN REBVS HVMANIS, CVI AETERNITAS OMNIS, TOTIVSQVE MVNDI NOTA SIT MAGNITVDO. CICERO.

2. The Spaniards Reach Mexico

Columbus was followed by other Spaniards. Columbus had wanted to find things out, but these people wanted to seize new lands for the Spanish King and Queen. Land, gold and other riches would make Spain powerful and wealthy.

The captains and sailors knew that the King would reward them well. Often he let them keep much of the gold and land for themselves. This meant that they could set up farms and use the local people as slaves.

Look for the natives fleeing from the Spaniards.

The new lands.

8

By the start of the 16th century the Spaniards were ruling Cuba, Haiti and other islands in the West Indies. The Spaniards made the natives give up their gods and turn to Christianity. This was the Spaniards' own religion, and they felt that they should fight to make others believe it too. They sometimes called themselves *Soldiers of Christ*. They were not just being greedy for land and gold: they were doing what they thought God wanted.

In 1519 a Spaniard called Hernán Cortés sailed from Cuba to Yucatán (now part of Mexico). He waved a special flag as he went on board his ship. The words were in Latin (the language people in Europe used for reading and writing).

AMICI SEQUAMOR CRUCEM ET SI NOS FIDEM HABEMUS VERE IN HOC SIGNO VINCEMUS

Cortés' flag. The words meant, "Friends, let us follow the cross, and if we have faith we will surely conquer in this sign".

The sign of the cross

Look at the picture of Cortés' flag and read the passage at the top of page 8.

1. What were the Spaniards' two main aims when they sailed to new countries?

2. The cross was a sort of badge for the Spaniards' religion. What was their religion called?
3. How did the Spaniards treat people who had other religions?
4. Discuss the meaning of Cortés' flag. Think of another way of saying the same thing. You could draw a flag and put your own words on it.

Hernán Cortés.

Andres de Tapia was one of Cortés' companions when he sailed to Mexico in 1519. Tapia wrote about what they found when they reached a small island.

This island had about 2 000 natives ... who worshipped idols and killed things to make the idols happy. One of the idols was in a high tower at the edge of the sea. The idol was made of baked clay and was hollow inside. It was fixed against a wall, and it looked as if a man could go round the back and get inside through a secret entrance ...The Indians said that the idol spoke.

At the foot of the tower the natives offered quail (a bird) and the blood of quail, and they burnt the sap of special trees to make a sweet smell. They said they did this when they needed rain, and that rain always fell soon afterwards.

Cortés called all the natives together. He begged them to tear down their idols, and they seemed to do so willingly. Then he had (Christian) crosses put up all over the island, and at the tower.

Cortés did not speak the natives' language, but one of the Spaniards knew it well. This Spaniard had joined Cortés' men when they arrived at the island. He explained that he and some other Spaniards had been shipwrecked there about 10 years earlier. One of his shipmates was married to a native, but the rest had died. The married Spaniard refused to join Cortés, pointing out that his ears were pierced and his hands and face were tattooed.

The Aztecs were the main tribe in Mexico. Above and below you can see two of the figures they made and worshipped.

? Worshipping idols

Read what Tapia wrote about the natives and their religion.

1. Pretend that you are Tapia and finish the following sentences:
   They said the idols spoke but ...
   They said their gods sent rain but ...
   They said the idols were important but ...
2. How can you tell that the Spaniards examined the tower very closely? How might the natives have felt about this?
3. Which are more reliable: reports by people who saw things happen (witnesses) or reports written later? Why do you think so?
4. Perhaps you cannot always trust witnesses. Tapia says that the natives changed their idols for crosses but another witness does not mention it. Do you think this part of Tapia's story is likely to be true? Why do you think so?

Pierced ears and tattoos

Look again at the top of this page.

1. Why did the Spaniard stay on the island?
2. Can you think of people who have to make this sort of decision today?

Life as a native

Pretend that you are one of the natives.

1. Write your own account of how the Spaniards treated your gods. Use Tapia's report to help you.
   Perhaps your work will start something like this:
   About 2 000 of us live on the island. We worship our gods by giving them some of our favourite food ...

They treat the beans as Spanish people treat silver and gold, and they use them as coins.

Pods of the cocoa tree.

3. Food and Drink

Cortés sailed right round the coast of Yucatán and landed where the city of Veracruz now stands. At that time, there was a native village on the shore. The villagers did not seem to have much treasure, but they had all kinds of food the Spaniards had not seen before. The Spaniards must have been eager to try it after the dull, unpleasant food they had eaten at sea.

Tapia tells an interesting story which shows us what the Spaniards usually ate:

We caught a shark with a hook and some ropes, but we could not haul it up because the ship would have tipped over, so we got in a skiff (small boat) and killed it in the water; then we cut it up and hauled it aboard in pieces. It turned out that the shark had eaten all the men's meat rations which had been tied to lines and left over the sides of the ship to soak. Inside the shark we found more than 30 sides of pork, a cheese, two or three shoes and a tin plate. The plate must have fallen overboard with the cheese. Although it had been in the shark's stomach we ate the pork because it tasted less salty than usual.

The men must have eaten the shark as well as the pork from inside it. Fresh fish was a treat. Most of their food was dry, hard, stale and salty to prevent it from going bad in the hot weather.

Food at sea

Read Tapia's story of the food eaten at sea.

1. Why were the sailors soaking their meat?
2. Why did they take salty meat with them?
3. What fresh meat could they get at sea?

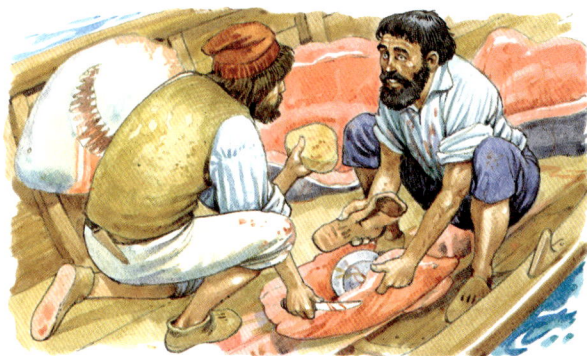

The natives gave the Spaniards food as a way of being friendly. In one place they gave them cooked turkey; in another they gave them fruit and maize.

Maize was one of the Aztecs' most important crops, but the Spaniards had never heard of it. The seeds are the edible part of the plant. When the Spaniards saw them they thought they were little peas!

The natives sent the Spaniards 20 slaves, who showed them how to grind the seeds into flour between stones. They added water and shaped the dough into little flat cakes. These were baked on special flat bricks or steamed in a cooking pot. Roughly ground maize was used to make porridge.

Nowadays most people eat maize. It is used to make cornflakes and other foods. We also make the little flat cakes the Aztecs used to make. We call them tortillas.

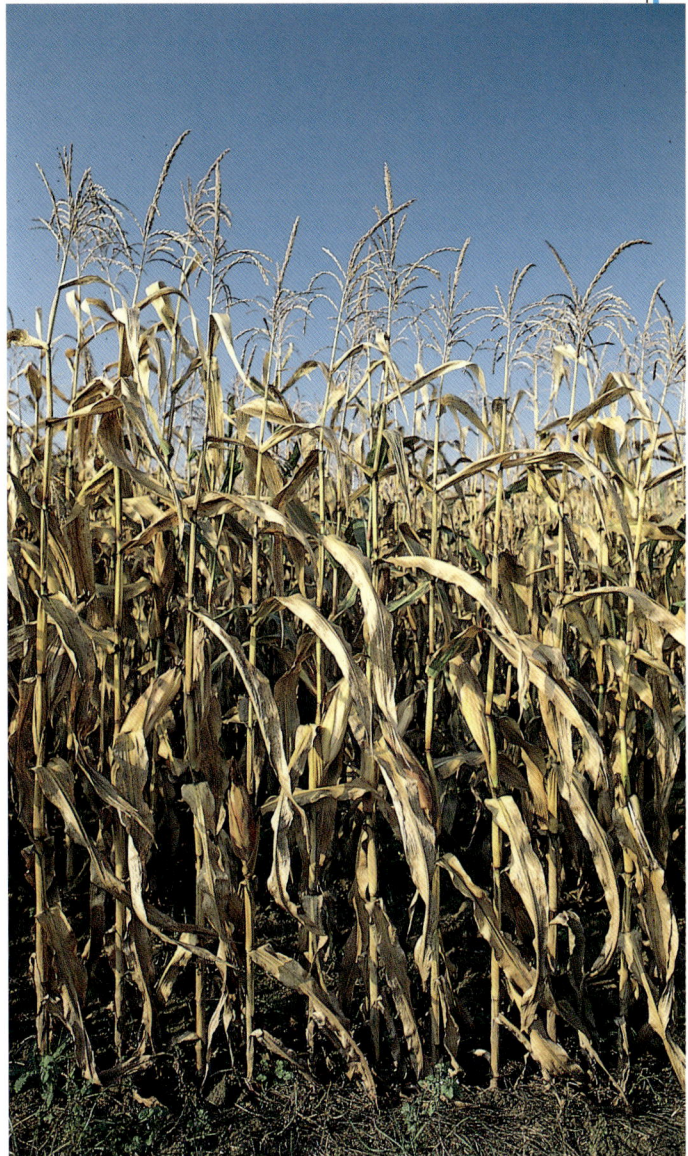

Where in the world is maize grown today?

Do you recognise these snacks made from maize?

◄ **What did the sailors find the shark had been eating?**

Cooking for Cortés

Pretend that you are the cook on board Cortés' ship, anchored just off the coast of Mexico. We know that Cortés "dined heartily", and we also know that he was "not fussy about his food, but he liked a good meal on special occasions".

1. Work out a meal for a special occasion which you can make from local foods. (You will have to send someone ashore for supplies.)
2. Design an attractive menu to go on Cortés' table to describe your meal.

The natives gave the Spaniards vegetables which they had never seen before. One was the sweet potato. This is like an ordinary potato but the Spaniards had never seen any sort of potatoes. They thought the sweet potatoes were like carrots.

How did the Aztecs make their drink from the "prickly bush"?

One of the sailors, called Díaz, wrote about another new vegetable:

Yucca are grown in mounds of earth and look like turnips. The roots are poisonous and harmful until they are chopped up and cooked in a special way. They can then be scraped, crushed and baked to make a sort of bread.

A Spaniard described another plant which the natives made a drink from:

It is a prickly bush that has leaves the thickness of a knee and the length of an arm ... From its centre sprouts a trunk as high as three men and as thick as a child of six or seven. At a certain time each year ... they bore a hole at the bottom and get the juice ... After a day or two they drink it ... and they do not stop until they fall to the ground drunk and senseless. They consider this a great honour.

They also make wine, vinegar and syrup from it; also men's and women's clothing and shoes, as well as cord, house beams, roof tiles and needles for sewing and stitching up wounds, and many other things.

Where would you find the edible part of this yucca?

The natives drank a lot of cocoa. They collected the cocoa beans, ground them up and added cold water. Then they beat the mixture with spoons to make it frothy.

Favourite drinks

Read the description of the natives' drinks and look at the photographs.

1. What sort of plant was the "prickly bush"?
2. Why do you think the Spaniards did not use its proper name?
3. The Spanish writer tells us some of the things the natives made from the prickly bush. Which pieces of the plant do you think they were made from?
4. What shows the natives' skill in medicine?

14

One of the native tribes was called the Aztecs. The Aztecs were more advanced than other tribes. They drew and painted beautiful pictures.

This page shows some Aztec pictures explaining what the weather (or the gods) could do to the soil and the maize in different years.

The Aztecs

Read about the Aztecs and study their paintings.

1. There are two figures in each picture. The one on the right is an Aztec god. What do you think the other figure is meant to be? How can you tell?

2. Do you think the Aztecs grew the maize, the yuccas and the "prickly bushes" themselves, or do you think they found them growing wild? Why do you think so?

3. The Aztecs worried about how the weather would affect their crops. The weather affects the crops we grow in Britain today but it worries us less. Discuss this difference and try to think of some reasons for it.

Each page gleams like a jewellery box that is shaken to make a fresh pattern of colours.

Deerskin pages of an Aztec codex.

4. Aztec Books

The Aztecs did not have books like ours. Instead of paper they used animal skins or the bark from trees. There were twelve stages in making an Aztec book:

The Aztecs shot deer or other animals with bows and arrows.

They sliced off the skins.

They stripped bark from trees.

They soaked the skins to stop them going bad.

▲ *They beat the skins or bark with hammers which made the material soft and smooth.*

They cut it into lengths, which they joined together to make a long roll. ▼

They coated it in white paint.

They painted the pictures using colours obtained from shells, cacti, beetles, petals, shellfish, soot and oil, chalky stones, leaves, rocks and clay.

They added black outlines.

▲ *They scratched the roll where they wanted to fold it.*

They folded it backwards and forwards. ▼

They added covers at each end.

The feel of a codex

Think about the feel, look and smell of an Aztec book, and the sound and puff of air it would make when you closed it.

1. Imagine that you are handling one for the first time and write a paragraph describing some of the things you notice.

Making an Aztec book

Look at the pictures explaining how the Aztecs made a book.

1. The Aztecs painted their books with brushes. How do you think they made the brushes?
2. The Aztecs added black outlines with a sort of pen. What do you think the pens were made of?
3. Why do you think the Aztecs scratched the picture roll before they folded it?
4. Study the photograph. Did the Aztecs use both sides of the page?
5. What do you think the covers of Aztec books were made from?

5. Paying Lord Montezuma

Cortés had not yet met the Aztecs who lived in the centre of Mexico but he had heard of them. He asked the natives questions about them. They said that the Aztecs were ruled by a man called Montezuma. They lived in the city of Tenochtitlan, which was built on an island and they made war on the rest of Mexico. Those who gave in peacefully had to pay heavy taxes; those who were beaten in battle were turned into slaves.

How long do you imagine one sack of raw cocoa would last an Aztec family?

Priests burnt incense in a burner like this. Look for the turkey claw decoration.

The natives did not like Montezuma's taxes but they had to pay them. They did not have money, so payments were always made in goods.

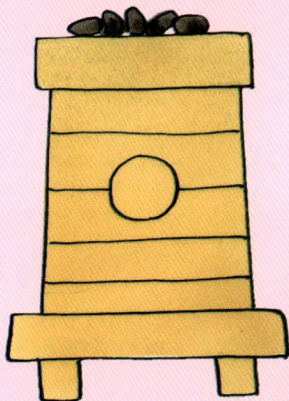

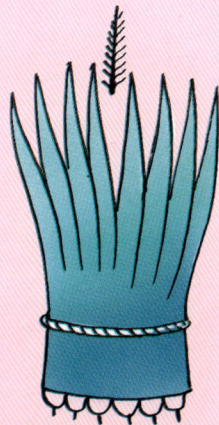

The Aztecs recorded the taxes paid to them by other tribes. Can you recognise these goods?

Life-size mask of an Aztec sun god. What are the teeth made from?

In the box below, is a list of the things one tribe had to send Montezuma in a year. It is a tax list.

2 400 loads of cloth, cut into large pieces for people to wear

800 loads of embroidered cloth, cut into small pieces

5 suits made of feathers, to protect chiefs in battle

60 suits made from feathers, to protect ordinary warriors in battle

40 suits for wearing in battle, with the feathers arranged in a special pattern

1 chest of beans

5 chests of maize

8 000 boxes of paper (made from the bark of a tree)

2 000 loaves of very white salt, for use by the lords of Mexico only

8 000 lumps of copal (incense) for burning in front of idols

(Adapted from an unascribed source in *The Conquistadors,* H. Innes, Collins 1986.)

Describe this pennant worn by a high priest.

Detective work

The tax list gives us information on what the Aztecs owned, what they ate and what things they thought were valuable. Read the list carefully.

1. What was the Aztecs' favourite drink?
2. What foods does the tax list mention?
3. What things in the list could the Aztecs wear or turn into clothes?
4. How did Aztecs make themselves look rich, important or beautiful?
5. What metals did the Aztecs use?
6. What is the name of the hardened sap the Aztecs burnt in front of their idols? Why do you think they wanted to make scented smoke?
7. How can we tell that the Aztecs did a lot of writing or drawing?
8. Suggest some things that the Aztecs might have used their axes for.
9. When they collected taxes, were Aztec officials more interested in ordinary things like food, or fine things like gold? How can you tell? Why do you think this was?
10. Try to find out what cochineal, amber and lime are. What might the Aztecs have used them for?

400 small baskets of best white copal

100 copper axes

80 loads of ordinary cocoa

800 cups (used for drinking cocoa)

1 little container, made of small turquoise stones

4 000 loads of lime

1 load of gold tiles, as thick as a finger

40 bags of cochineal

20 cases of gold dust

1 gold crown

20 lip jewels made of amber and gold

100 pots of liquid amber

8 000 handfuls of rich scarlet feathers

40 animal skins

1 600 bundles of cotton

What do you think would have been drunk from this cup?

6. Spaniards March Inland

The natives said that Montezuma's capital city, Tenochtitlan, was built partly on land and partly on water. The Spaniards were puzzled, but they knew they would soon see the city for themselves. They began to march inland.

How would it have felt to have been part of the march to Tenochtitlan?

Tapia described what the march was like:

We left the natives, who had become our friends, and for a hundred kilometres or more we crossed the badlands; there were salt water lakes and we suffered from hunger but more from thirst. At last we reached a town called Zacollan. Cortés asked the lord of this town whether he was ruled by Montezuma, and he replied, 'And who can there be who is not a servant of this great lord?'

(A few days later) Cortés reached an idol house that had two or three little buildings around it, where we put our baggage ... Certain natives came to Cortés, bringing five other natives with them and saying, 'If you are a god that eats meat and blood, eat these men and we shall bring you more. And if you are a kind god, here are feathers and copal. And if you are a man, here are turkeys, maize, bread and cherries.'

The Aztecs used fine featherwork shields for ceremonies and battles.

(After several days marching) we reached the city of Cholula, and Cortés sent a number of men to explore a smoking volcano we could see. Meanwhile, Montezuma's messengers came to see us in the city. They said that Montezuma would die of fright if we went to see him. They also said that Montezuma had lions and tigers and other wild beasts that he could let loose on us.

Marching to Tenochtitlan

Read the description of the march given by Tapia.
1. Tapia mentions the "badlands". What was bad about them?
2. List three things the natives thought Cortés might be. In each case, say what they brought as a present.
3. What things were meant to be eaten?
4. The Spaniards had never seen a volcano. What do you think they thought of the one they saw on their journey?

? Entering the city

Look at the drawing of Spanish forces marching into Mexico on page 22.

1. Try to find some people who might be native Mexicans. What are they doing?
2. Why do you think they are helping the Spaniards?
3. What signs did the Spaniards put on their flags?
4. Why were these signs important to them?
5. Suggest which figure in the drawing might be Cortés. Why do you think so?

Imagining the great Montezuma

As they gathered around their camp-fires at night, the Spaniards discussed Montezuma and what sort of person he might be.

1. Imagine you are one of the Spanish soldiers. Make up a conversation between Tapia, Cortés and yourself. If you like, you can start with Cortés saying:
"Cunning, cowardly, powerful? Why can't you make up your minds?"

Native armies fought several battles against the Spaniards and one of the fiercest took place near Cholula. A Spaniard called Gomara described the battle (which the Spaniards won) and the natives' weapons and battledress:

The men were armed in their finest way. Their faces were painted with red dye, and they looked like devils. They carried plumes and moved about on the battlefield with amazing skill. Their weapons were slings, pikes, lances and swords; bows and arrows. They had helmets on their heads and wooden armour on their arms and legs. Their large and small shields, which were very fine and not at all weak, were of tough wood and leather, with brass and feather ornaments. Their wooden swords had flint set into them, which cut well and made a nasty wound.

This Aztec page tells us about their weapons.

They fought in large groups, each with many trumpets, conches and drums, all of which were a sight to see.

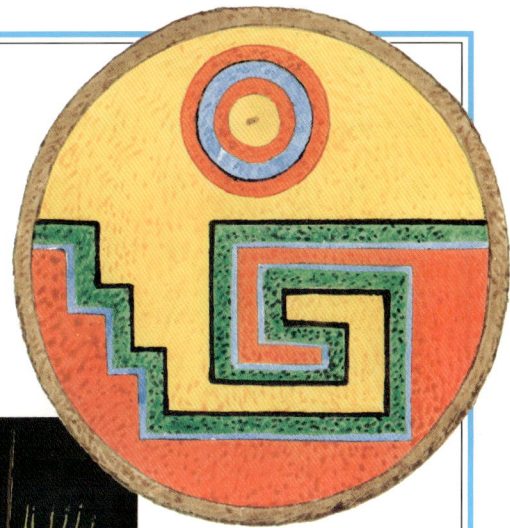

What materials have been used to make the shield, arrows and helmet?

❓ Warriors

Read the passage written by Gomara.

1. What does Gomara think of the natives' armour? What details seem to impress him most?
2. Why do you think the native soldiers painted their faces?
3. List the materials which Gomara mentions.
4. A conch is a natural object. Find out what it is and what it is used for.
5. Draw a native soldier with some of the weapons and other equipment Gomara mentions.

The city of Tenochtitlan, built on a huge lake.

Approaching the city we could see great towers and churches and large palaces and houses.

7. Entering Tenochtitlan

The Spaniards were soon in the Aztecs' part of Mexico. At last they reached a lake that had formed in the crater of an old volcano. Roads built on soil led across the lake, and there in the centre the Spaniards could see the gleaming city of Tenochtitlan.

The Spaniards left us detailed descriptions of Tenochtitlan. One of them wrote:

This great city is built in the salty part of a lake. It is joined to the land by three high roads built of stone and earth. Along one of these roads a canal has been built, bringing good fresh water from a mountain stream.

As the Spaniards marched into Tenochtitlan there were two lines of Aztec nobles coming to meet them.

According to a Spaniard called Aguilar:

Between them came the great King Montezuma, in a curtained throne. He could be seen by no one, and none of the Aztecs dared stare at the throne, which they carried on their shoulders. In front of Montezuma walked a man with a long mace in his hand, representing Montezuma's greatness.

When Cortés was within a stone's throw of Montezuma he got off his horse. Montezuma then appeared and placed necklaces of gold and precious stones about Cortés, and Cortés placed a string of painted beads about Montezuma's neck.

Charles V, King of Spain and the Holy Roman Emperor.

Montezuma swore in front of a scribe to obey and serve His Majesty Charles V. He said that word had been handed down from his ancestors that bearded and armed men were to come from where the sun rises and they were not to be attacked.

Look for the gifts exchanged between Montezuma and Cortés.

Tenochtitlan.

The Aztecs made necklaces similar to the two on these pages using gold and precious stones.

? Cortés and Montezuma

Use all the information in this chapter.

1. Whose gifts were worth more - the gifts Montezuma gave Cortés or the gifts Cortés gave Montezuma?
2. What might have been the reason for this?
3. What were the Aztecs' attitudes to Cortés? List four or five things in the passage which make this clear.
4. Copy the table and tick the box if you agree with the statement.

" According to Cortés, Montezuma said this:

You have come from where the sun rises. From this, and from what you tell us of your great lord or king who has sent you here, we firmly believe that he is our rightful sovereign (ruler).

" According to an Aztec, Montezuma said this:

I have met you face to face! I was in agony for five days, for ten days, with my eyes fixed on the Region of the Mystery. And now you have come out of the clouds and mists to sit on your throne again. You have come back to us; you have come down from the sky.

How would Montezuma have felt in his head-dress?

28

Montezuma thinks the Spaniards are gods.	
Cortés is going to rule the Aztecs himself.	
Montezuma accepts the Emperor (Charles V) as his ruler.	
There was a scribe to take notes.	

Different opinions

There are three accounts in this chapter of the first meeting between Montezuma and Cortés.

1. Are there any differences between the three?
2. Discuss why people give different accounts of the same event. You could start by comparing what you and your friends say about something that has happened in your school or town. You could also compare reports in newspapers.
3. According to the Aztec, Montezuma spent five or ten days in agony with his eyes "fixed on the Region of the Mystery". Discuss the meaning of this with your friends.

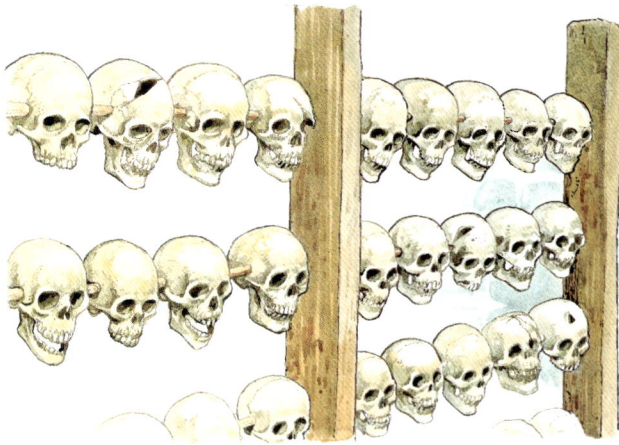

Feathers and gold inside and out; walls caked with blood, buzzing with flies; a bowl of human hearts; priests dancing and scenting the air with copal.

8. Holy Places in Tenochtitlan

The Spaniards were amazed when they entered the square in the centre of Montezuma's city.

According to Tapia:

There would have been space for 400 Spaniards to build their houses. (The square had) a huge stone platform with 113 steps (leading up it). On the top were two towers, and in one of these was the Aztecs' main god. He was made from all kinds of seeds, which had been ground and mixed up with boys' and girls' blood, making a shape which was fatter than a man and just as tall. On feast days they put gold jewellery ... and very fine clothes on the figure.

There was also a second platform with towers, but Tapia does not say how high it was. Perhaps he forgot because he was so surprised to see thousands of skulls staring from it. Between the towers there were 60 or 70 tall wooden posts, and from top to bottom they were linked together with wooden rods. This made a rack for the skulls. The Aztecs had bored two holes in each skull, and they had pushed five skulls on to every rod. Tapia and another Spaniard worked out that there were 136 000 skulls altogether.

Tapia wondered where all the skulls might have come from, and he asked Montezuma why he and his captains did not wipe out a troublesome tribe. Montezuma replied:

We could easily do so. But then we would have nowhere to train our youths except in far away places. Also, we wish to have people at hand to sacrifice to our gods.

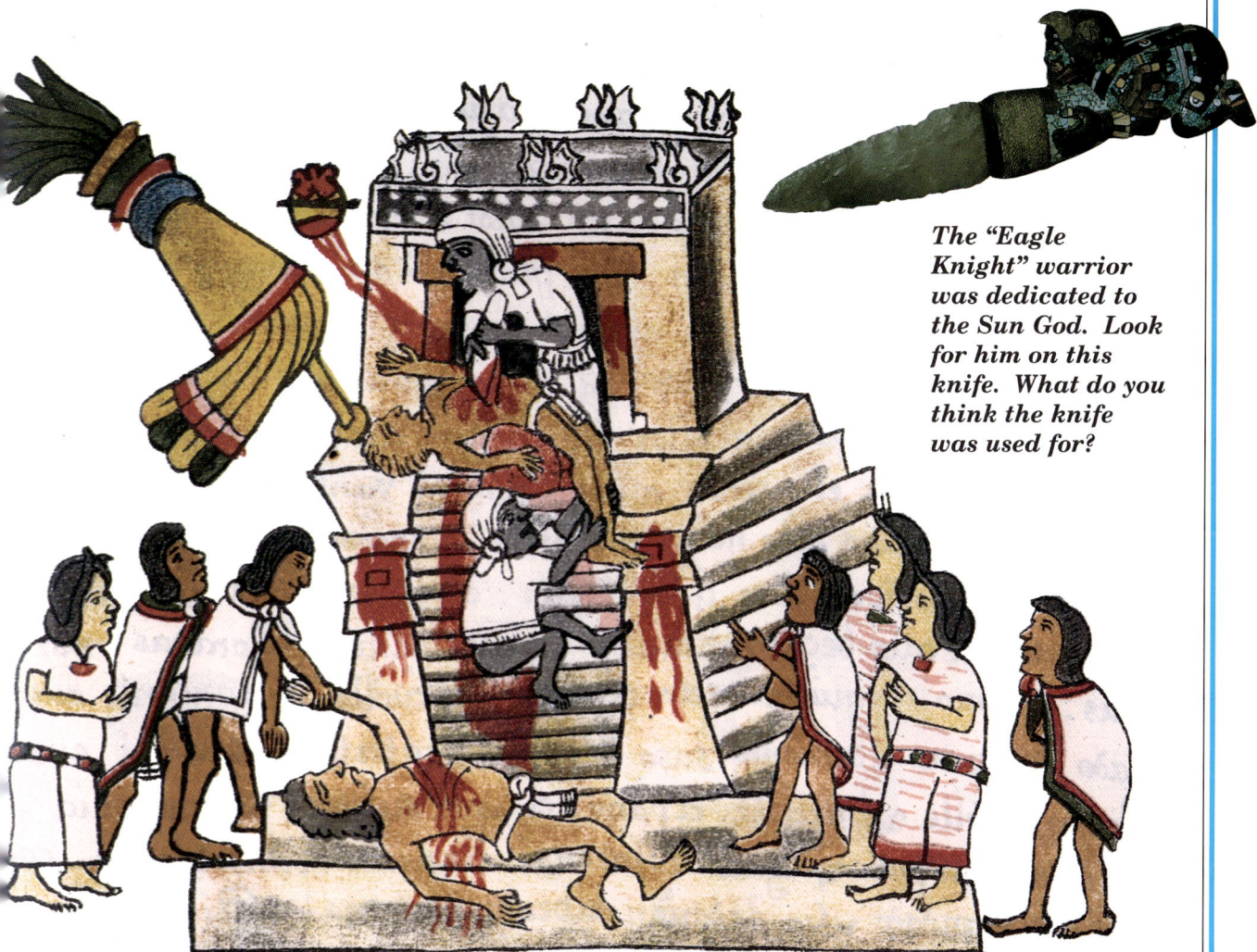

The "Eagle Knight" warrior was dedicated to the Sun God. Look for him on this knife. What do you think the knife was used for?

A sacrifice to the Sun God.

A sacrifice

Look at the picture showing an Aztec priest and two victims.

1. Which is the priest and which are the victims?
2. What is the priest doing?
3. What is the man on the steps doing?
4. The idol in one of the towers was the Aztecs' god of rain. Why do you think this god was important?

5. Find the heart and say why you think the artist drew it in the air.
6. The artist was an Aztec himself, and he drew his picture shortly after the Spaniards had taken his country over. Do you think he is likely to give us a good picture of Aztec life? Why?
7. According to Tapia, the statue of the god was made from certain things. What were they and why do you think they were chosen?
8. Pretend that you are the priest in the picture. Use your own words to explain why Montezuma did not wipe out the troublesome tribe.

Clay models of the temples survive today giving us clues about their appearance.

Archaeologists are people who study things that remain from the past. They have many questions about the Aztecs' towers or temples. Did each tribe have its own sort of tower - or several sorts? Did styles of building change with timc? Did people pass on old ideas and change them accidentally?

Only one Aztec temple still survives. Bodies were sacrificed on the platform and rolled down the steps to soften the flesh for eating. Look for the two bowls where great fires burned.

Were writers and artists sometimes careless about what they said or showed in their work? Did writers and artists sometimes exaggerate or try to mislead others?

Archaeologists now know a lot about the temples in Mexico even though most have fallen down or been destroyed. Clues have come from: the places where temples stood; pictures of the temples; models made for people to keep in their homes; and Spanish descriptions of the temples.

A Spaniard called Juan Díaz landed on the Mexican coast and described an idol room "eight spans wide and the height of a man". He did not mention any platform. Tapia said that the towers in Tenochtitlan were higher than a pike and a half and stood on huge platforms.

The trouble with having all these clues is that sometimes they seem to disagree.

What designs decorated the temples?

Investigating historical evidence

Look at the things in this chapter that tell you (or show you) what Aztec temples were like.

1. The clues give different ideas about what the towers were like. What are the most important differences?
2. Discuss why the clues differ in what they tell us about the towers.
3. Do you think the towers at Tenochtitlan were round or square? You will have to decide which clues can be trusted and which cannot.

Measuring and comparing

Think about what you have read in this chapter.

1. Why do you think the Spaniards talked about pikes and spans instead of using measurements like metres?
2. How did people use their bodies to measure things before they had rulers?
3. Who do you think destroyed the temples? Why?
4. What do we call people who dig up and study clues from the past?
5. Think about two schools or churches, one old and one new, near where you live. Try to describe how the buildings differ.

There were over 100 000 houses in the city, each built over the water on wooden posts like a fortress and with roof tops full of people.

A plan of an Aztec palace.

9. Fine Houses

The Spaniards were amazed when they saw Tenochtitlan.

Inside a palace

Look at the picture above.

1. Find the room where a king and his son are talking.
2. Find the central courtyard. What are the people doing here?

This is what a Spaniard wrote about the streets and houses:

The streets are wide and beautiful. Two or three of the main ones are built on an island but the rest are half water and half banks of soil. The people walk on the soil or ride canoes on the water. The canoes are dug out of tree trunks, and some are large enough to hold five people easily.

There are other streets which are all water, so people have to go by canoe. Without their canoes they would not be able to get to their houses.

The houses belonging to the lords were so large and had so many rooms that they were amazing to see.

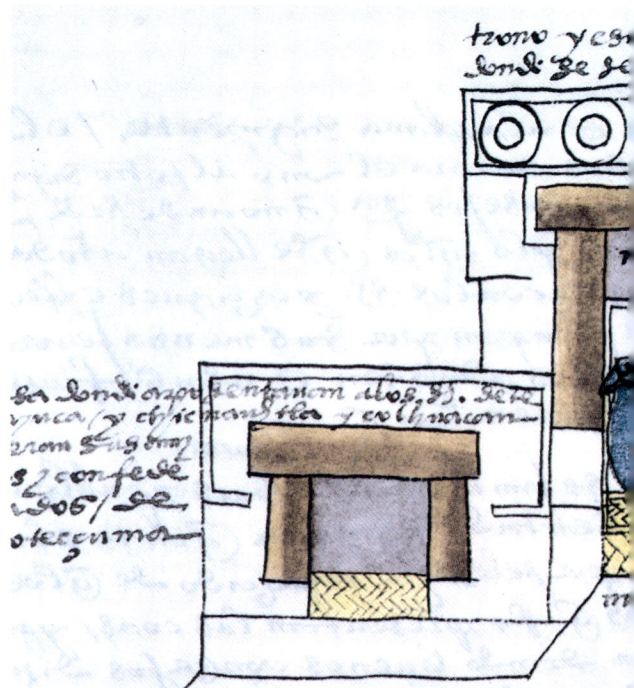
Montezuma in his palace. A Spaniard has

Montezuma's palace

Look at the picture showing part of Montezuma's main palace in peace time.

1. Do you think the palace was built of wood or stone? What clues help you?
2. Which do you think gives a better idea of the size of Montezuma's palace - the Spaniards' descriptions (right) or the Aztec's drawing?
3. The Spaniards were frightened when they saw Montezuma's animals gnawing bones.

many people there were to look after them. From large clay jars came the rattling sound of snakes and vipers, helping to show Montezuma's importance, and he kept men and women who were crippled, deformed or had not grown properly.

He also kept every possible kind of water bird. I can swear that more than 600 men spent all their time looking after them. There was even a special place for sick birds. With the water birds Montezuma kept people whose eyebrows, hair and bodies were completely white.

According to a Spaniard:

At one of his houses Montezuma kept cages of wolves, foxes, lions, tigers and other wild cats. There were also cages with birds of prey such as falcons and hawks. It amazed me to see how much meat they ate and how

Another Spaniard described the lords' houses like this:

It was the custom in all the lords' houses to have very large rooms and halls around a courtyard, and in one of the houses there was a hall large enough to hold more than 3 000 people comfortably. And the house was also so large that 30 men could have had a mock battle on the roof as if they were on a great square.

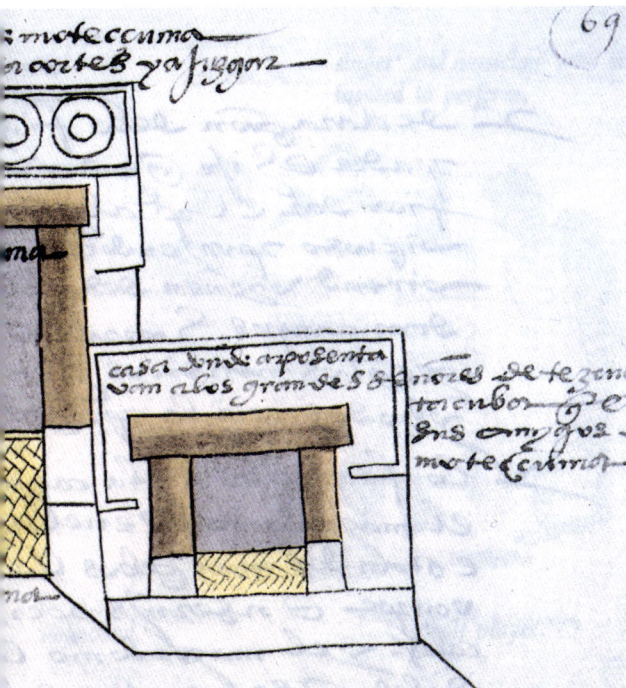

written notes on the picture.

City homes

Read the descriptions of the houses in Tenochtitlan.

1. Do you think all the houses were built on wooden posts?
2. Did the houses in Tenochtitlan have flat or sloping roofs? Why?
3. Do you think the temple in Tenochtitlan was built on land or over water? Explain your answer.

10. Dangerous Games

This ball court can still be seen in Mexico. Do you think clues about our football pitches will remain for archaeologists to discover in hundreds of years time?

The Aztecs played all sorts of games. One, which the Spaniards called volador (flying), was very risky. They took the trunk of a tall, straight tree and fixed it up in a village or town. They coiled 4 lengths of rope round the top and built a platform a little way down. The platform could spin round and round.

At the chosen time, 4 men dressed as birds climbed up to the platform. Someone tied the ropes round their waists and they jumped off. As soon as they did so, the ropes began to unwind from the post. The platform started going round and the men circled downwards, towards the ground. After 13 circles they finally skidded to a halt in the dust and everyone cheered.

The Aztecs also used poles and ropes in another way. They scrambled up them to reach and eat a sugary figure at the top. The figure was probably made to look like one of their gods.

Volador

Look at the picture of volador.

1. Why do you think there were ropes all the way up the volador pole?
2. The Aztecs thought about their gods when they watched volador. Try to decide why.
3. Pretend that you are one of the volador "bird men" and write about what it was like to take part. Remember the dangers.

Volador "gods".

Young men from rich families played a game called tlachtli. This was played on a court as big as a modern football pitch, with walls three times as high as the players. Fixed in the middle of each wall there was a stone ring. It was too high to reach, but the players had to knock a rubber ball through it using only their elbows, knees or thighs.

The game was fast and furious. The players were in two teams and they competed fiercely, diving for the ball on the hard stone floor. People watched excitedly from the tops of the walls, often betting on which team would win. If anyone scored, the players were allowed to rob the spectators, who would try to run away.

Trying to score at tlachtli.

A game of patolli.

The Aztecs also played a board game called patolli. It was rather like ludo, but with beans as dice and counters. To bring themselves luck, they spoke to the beans, rubbed them between their hands and burned incense. Some Aztecs would bet so much on patolli and other games that they got into debt and they had to sell themselves as slaves.

? Tlachtli

Read the description of tlachtli.

1. Do you think it was easy or hard to score?
2. How does the tlachtli court in the photograph differ from the court described in the text? Suggest a possible reason for the difference.
3. After a hard game of tlachtli, players must have had lots to say to each other. Finish the following sentences:

I fainted with thirst because ...
I felt terribly tired because ...
I wore padding because ...
I had bruises and cuts because ...
I was proud because ...
I was angry because ...
After scoring, I chased ...

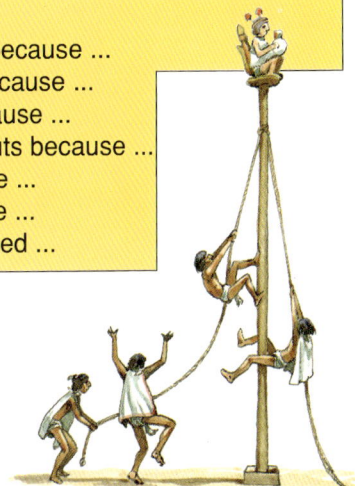

Climbing the greasy pole.

Masks

Cut two eye-holes in practically anything and you have a mask. It can be as simple or as complicated as you wish. Here are three masks made from cardboard egg-boxes decorated with wool. Attach a piece of elastic large enough to go round the head, making sure that the holes are not too near the edge.

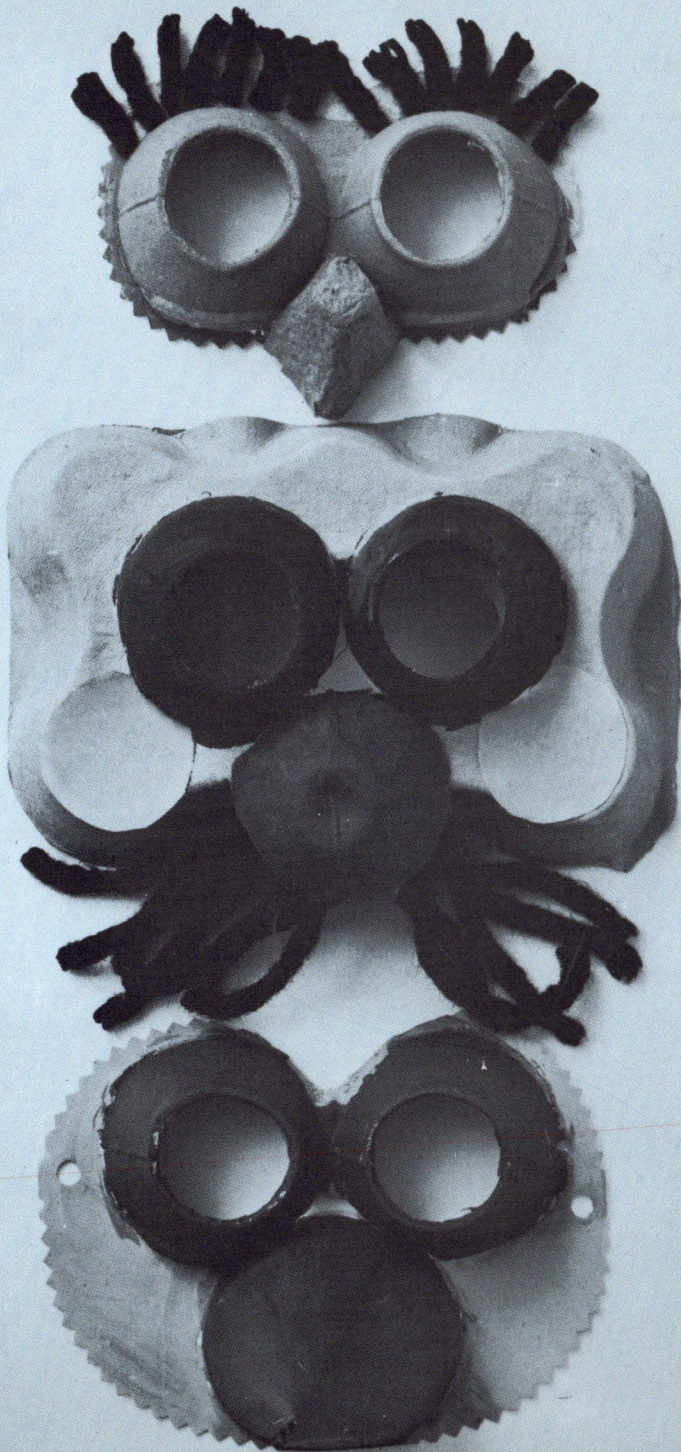

Decorated Paper Cups

A plain white paper cup is an ideal surface on which to make a funny face. Here are three suggestions for bringing your cups to life.

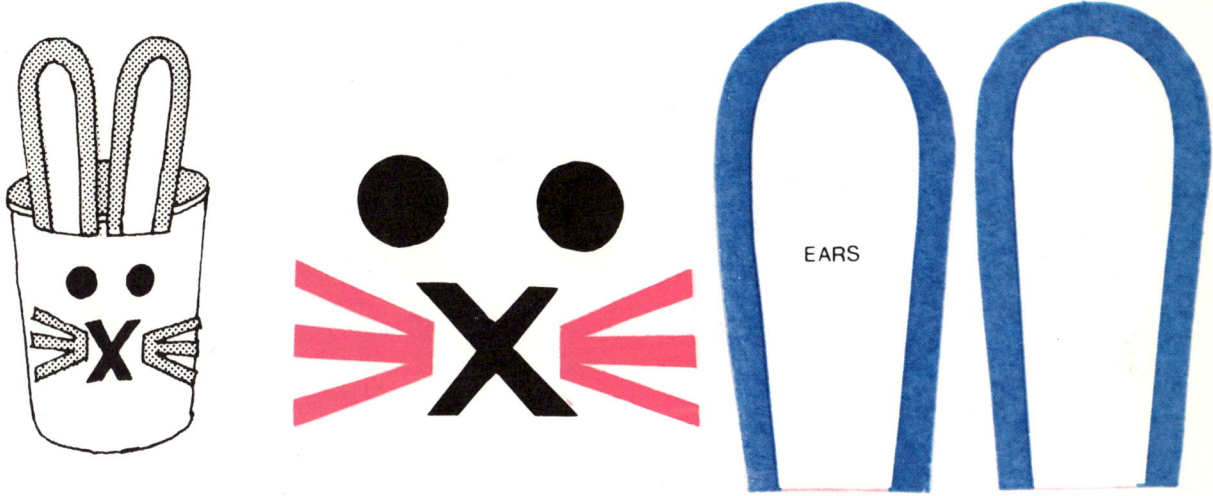

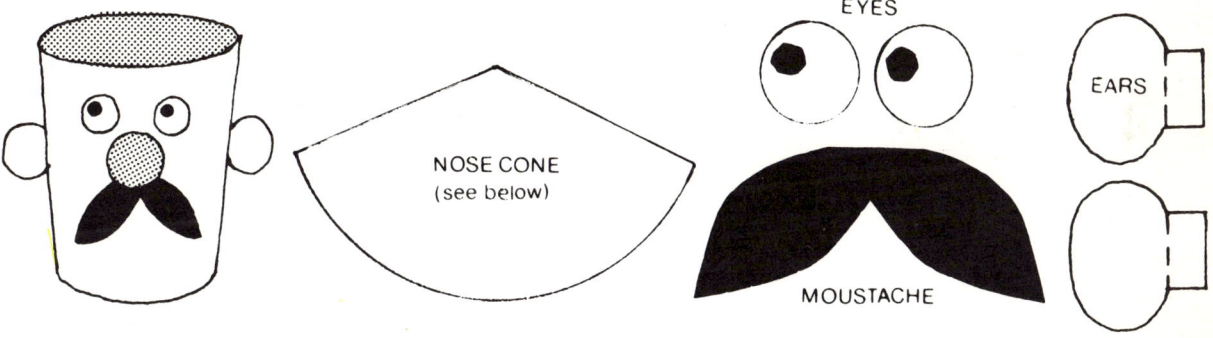

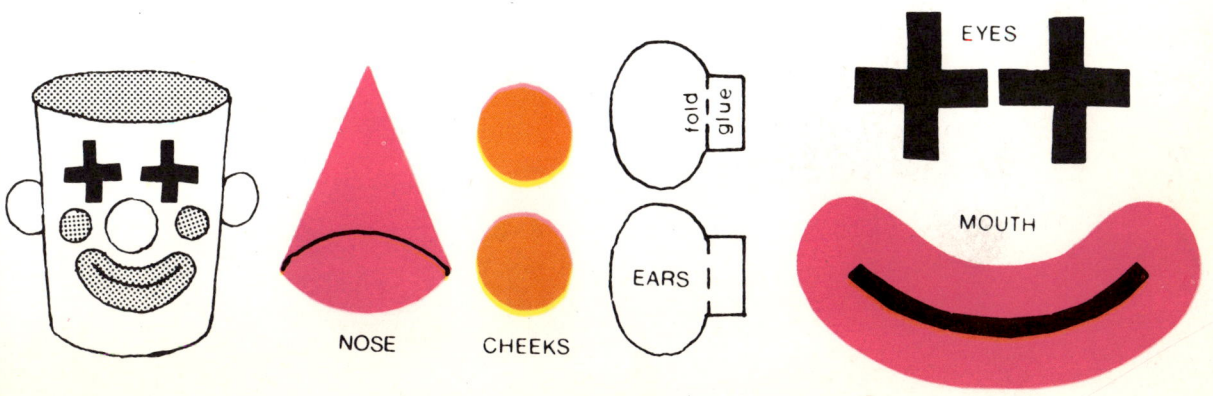

EARS

EYES

EARS

NOSE CONE
(see below)

MOUSTACHE

EYES

fold glue

EARS

MOUTH

NOSE

CHEEKS

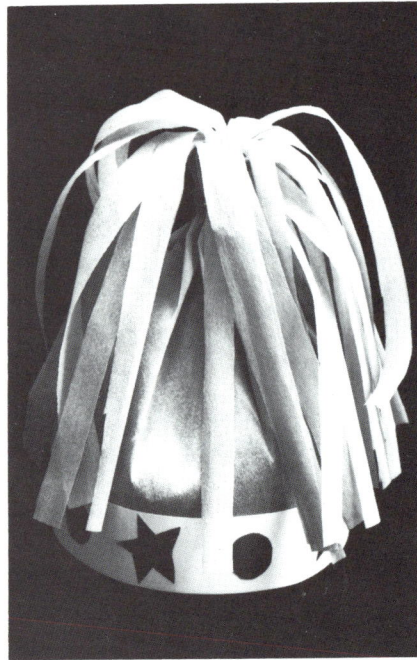

Hats

fold

cut

1 tissue paper

twist

2 card

3 stick to top

make cone

4

1 card

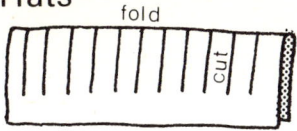

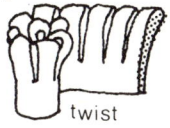

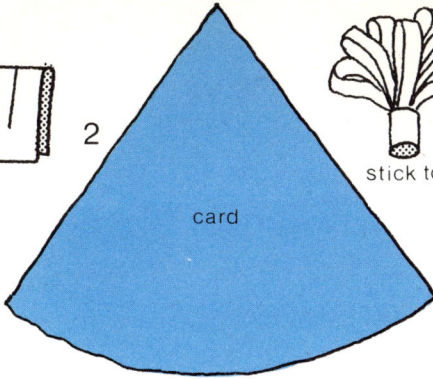

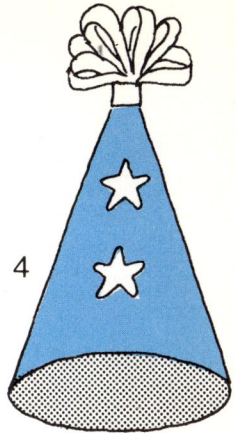

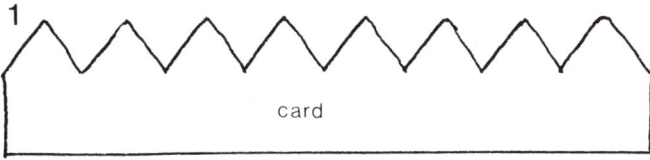

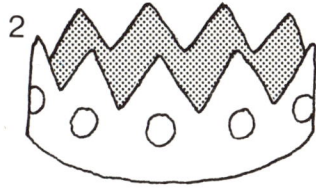

2 decorate with squashed milk bottle tops

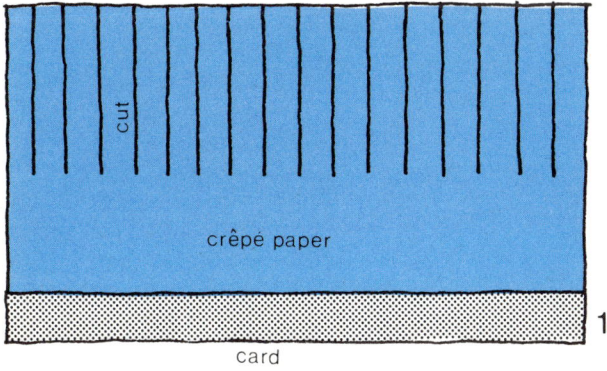

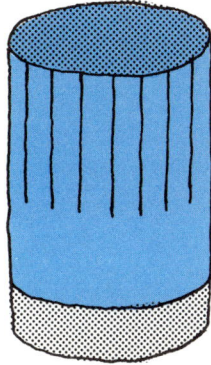

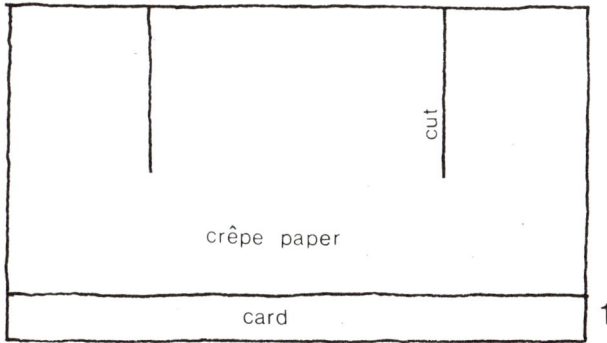

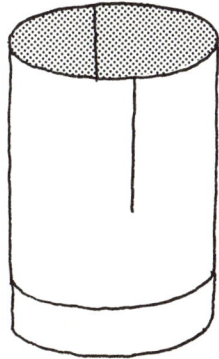

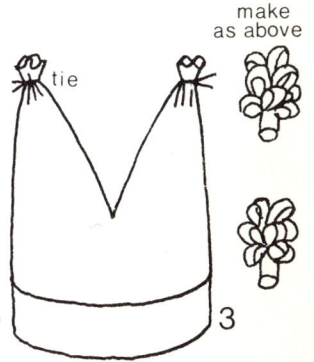

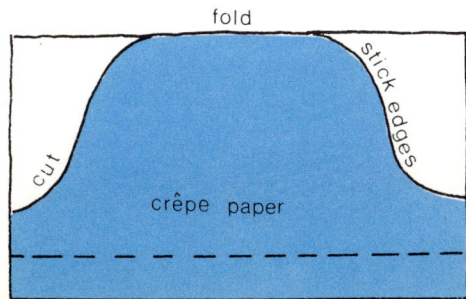

cut

crêpé paper

card 1

2

tie

3

cut

crêpe paper

card 1

tie

2

3

make as above

fold

stick edges

cut

crêpe paper

1

2

fold round strip of card

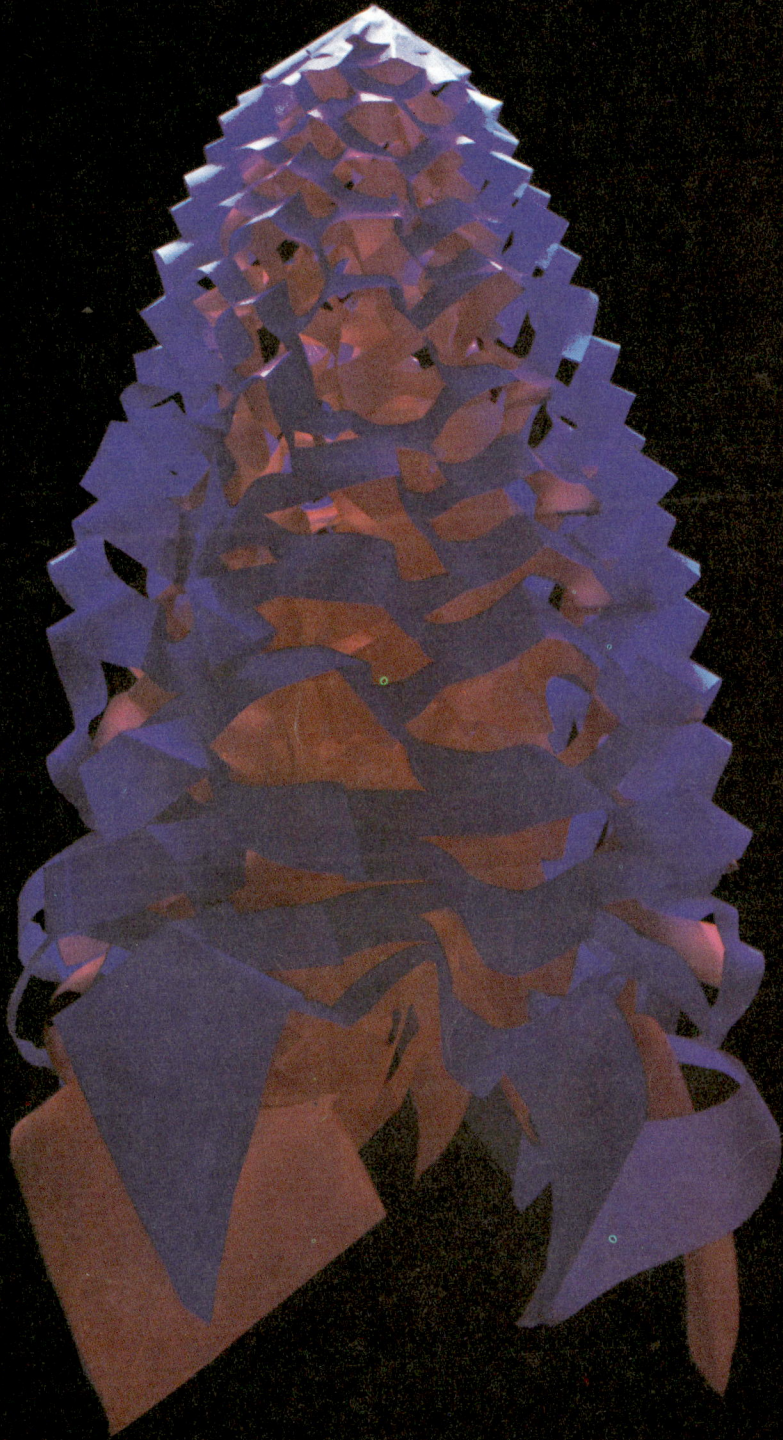

Rosette

For this hanging design (see page 30) it is best to use *origami* paper squares which come in packets. You will need six equal squares of different colours and some strips of tissue-paper for the 'tail'.

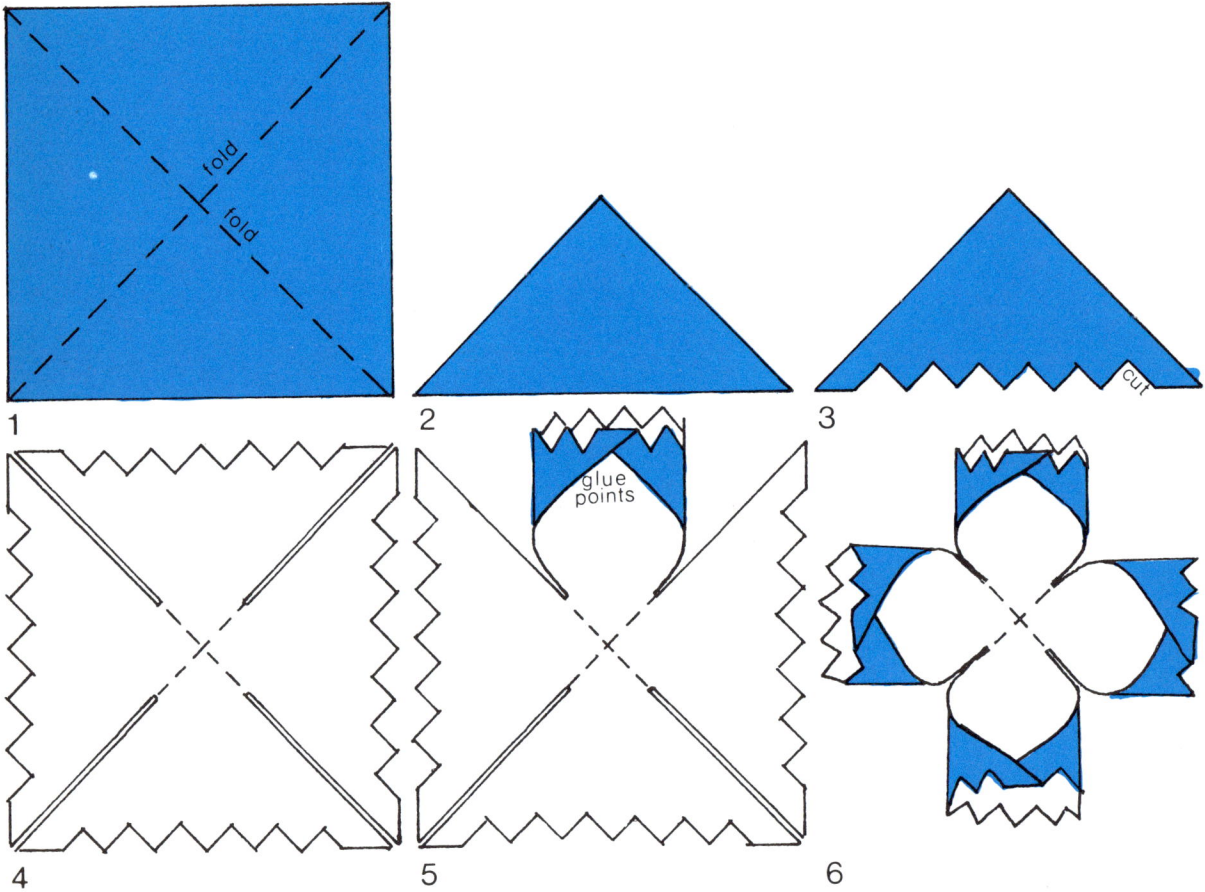

fold

fold

1

2

3

cut

glue points

4

5

6

Fold long tissue strips in half and tie at the fold with a piece of cotton. Then thread the other end of the cotton through the middle of each star, and pull firmly together. Secure with a piece of sticky tape wound round the cotton.

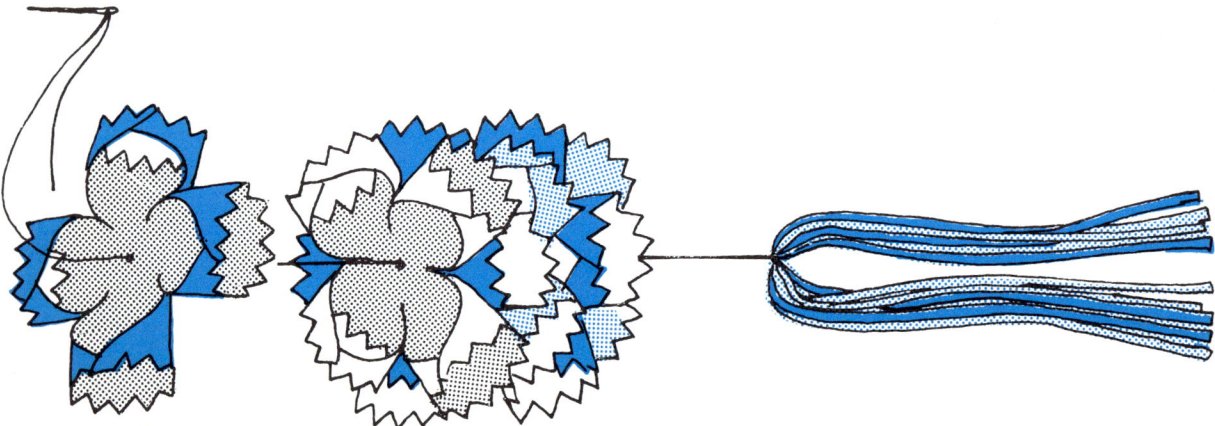

Waterfall

Use a square of coloured tissue-paper as large as possible. Fold four times as shown below and cut the folded paper so that each cut is more than half-way across. Carefully unfold the paper-cut. Put a small paper disc at the centre to take the weight of the tissue-paper when suspended. Through this cotton is then knotted and threaded. The photograph on page 31 shows two different-coloured waterfalls hanging one inside the other.

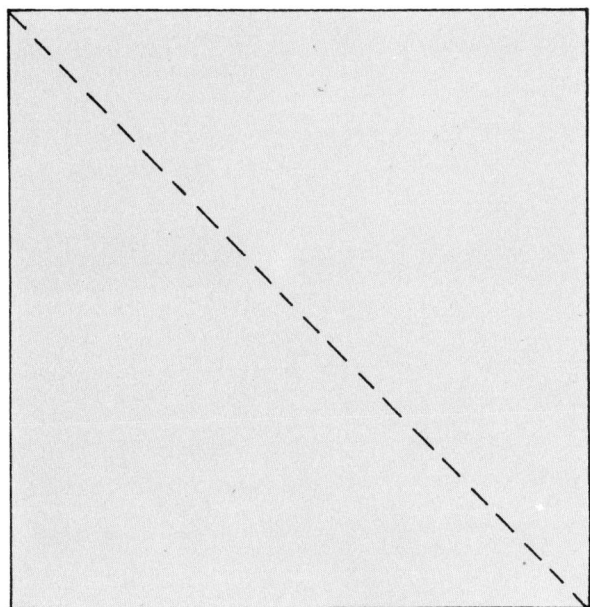

1

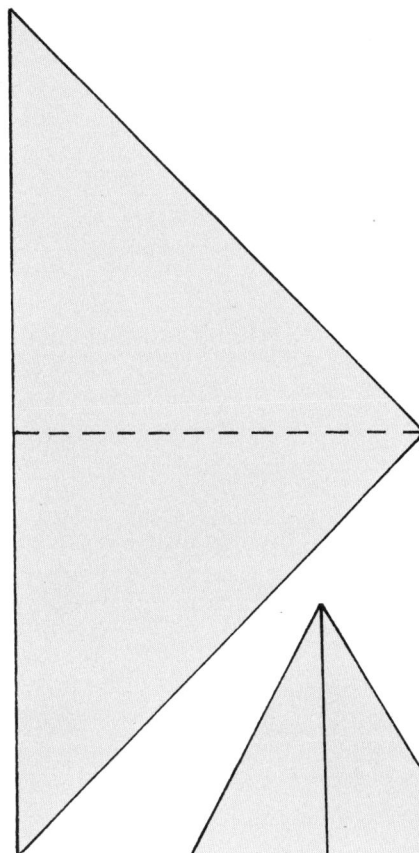

2

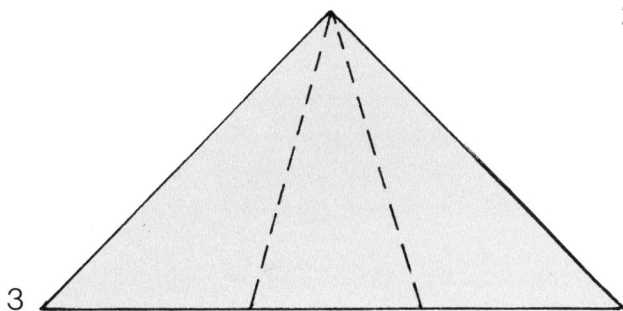

3

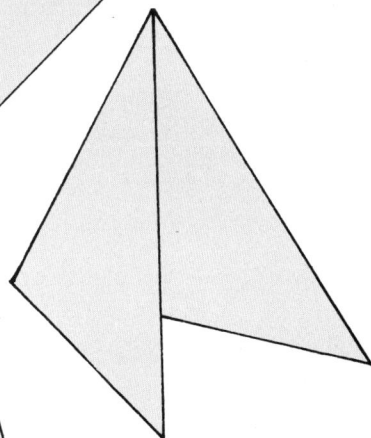

4

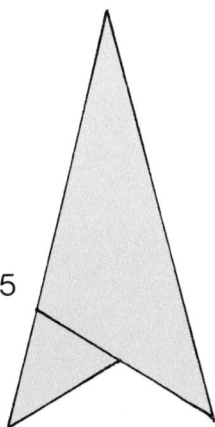

5

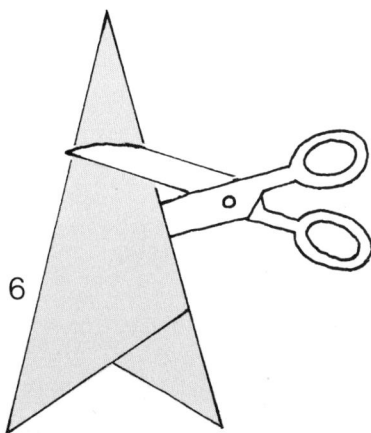

6

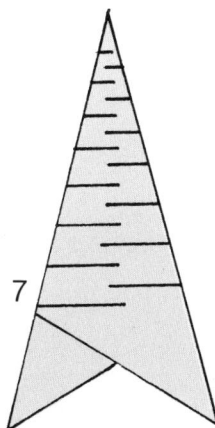

7

c

Star

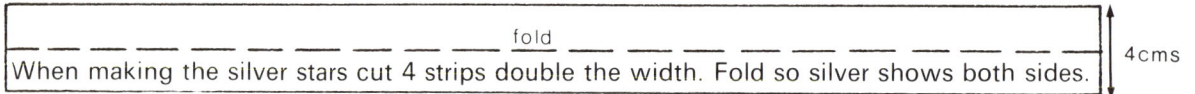

fold

When making the silver stars cut 4 strips double the width. Fold so silver shows both sides.

4 cms

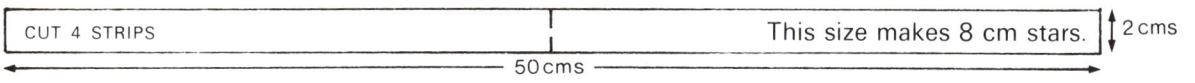

CUT 4 STRIPS

This size makes 8 cm stars.

2 cms

50 cms

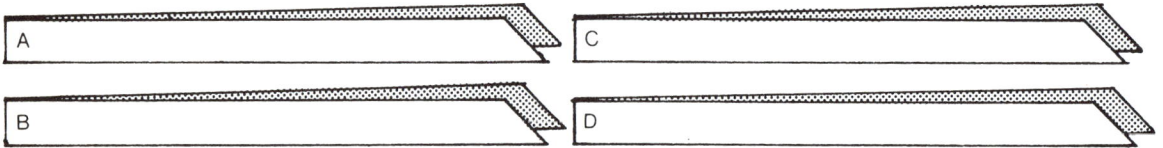

A

C

B

D

REPEAT 10–15
ON STRIPS B, C, AND D

16
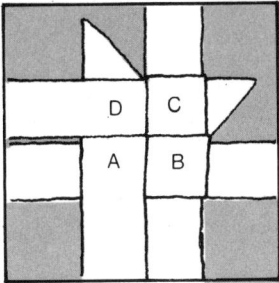

17
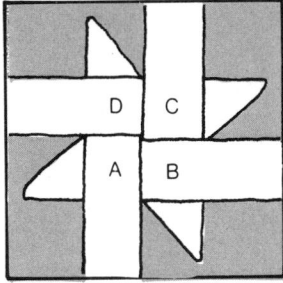

TURN OVER
AND COMPLETE
ALTERNATE POINTS
18–23
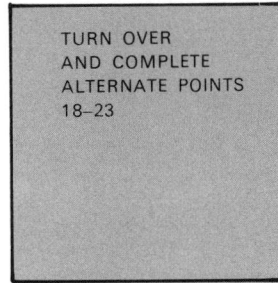

18
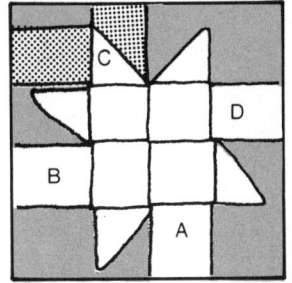

19
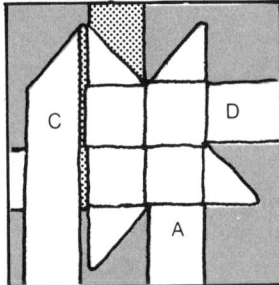

20
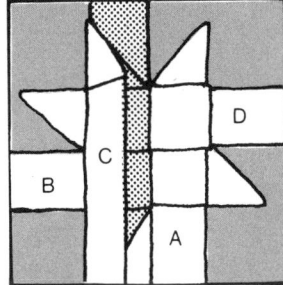

21
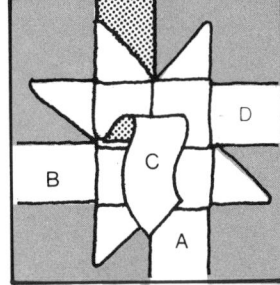

22
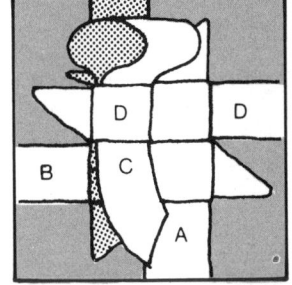

23
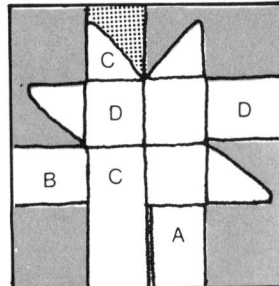

24
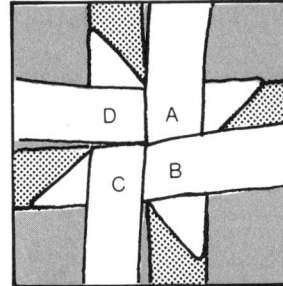

25
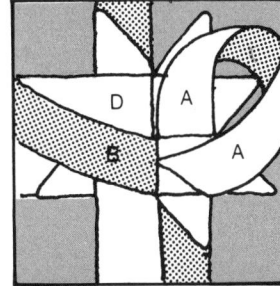

HOLD BACK *B*
TWIST UP *A* AND
THREAD THROUGH
UNDER *B* PULL END
OF *A* TIGHT TO FORM
POINT. REPEAT 18–23
TO FORM 4 POINTS.
TURN OVER AND
COMPLETE 4 MORE
POINTS 24–29. TRIM
ENDS WITH SCISSORS
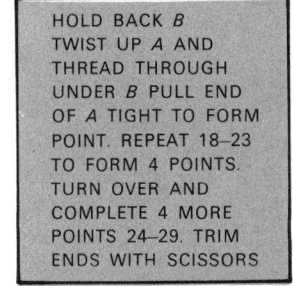

26
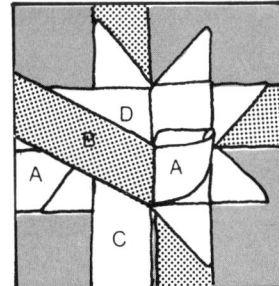

27
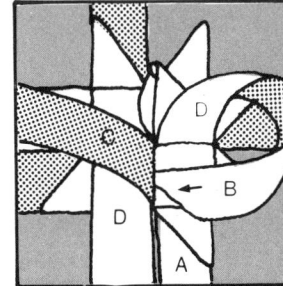

28
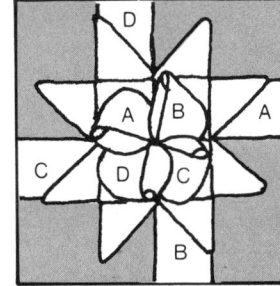

29
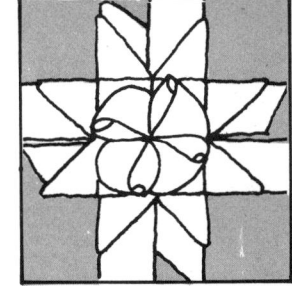

30
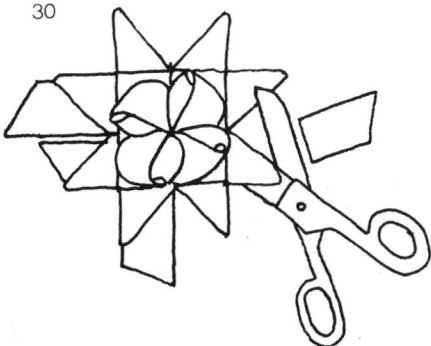

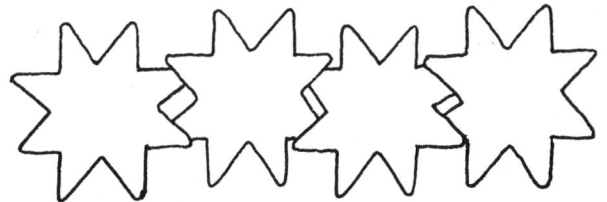

To make a garland 9 stars are needed. Stick together in the above way and join to form a circle. Make a larger star for the middle.

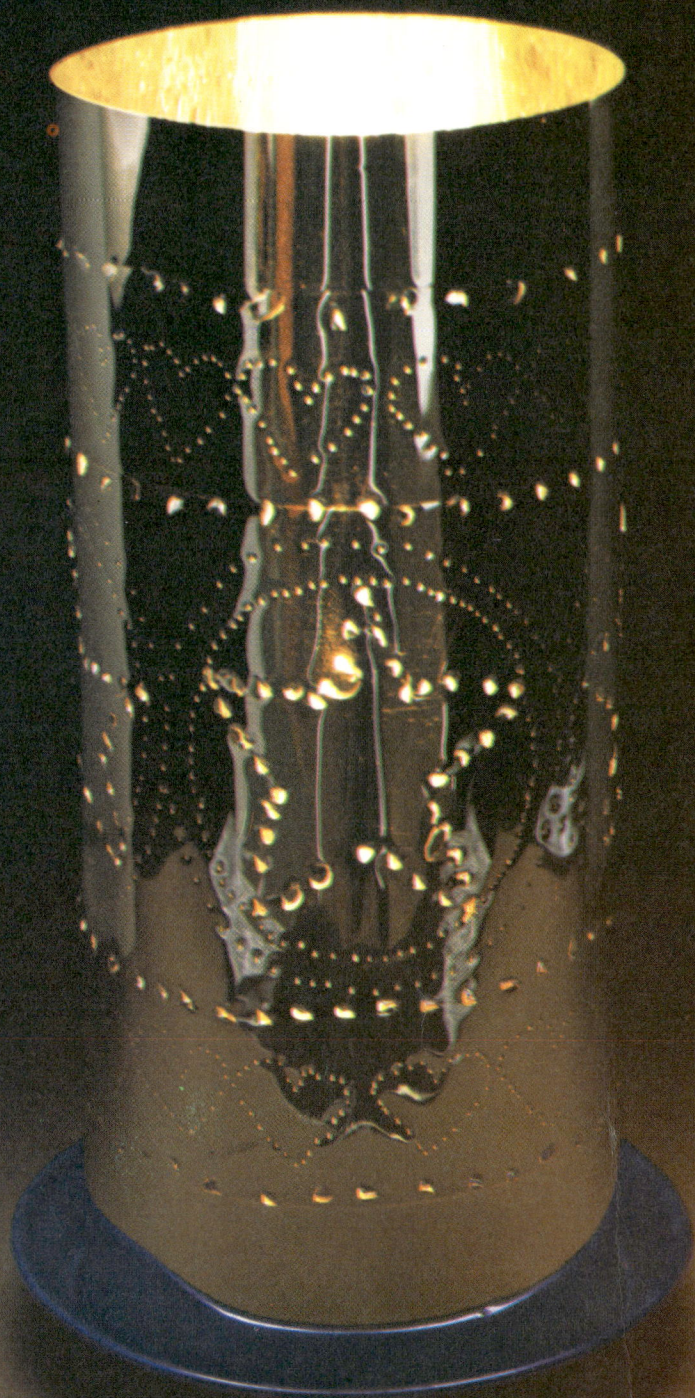

Candle Lamp

Use a piece of fairly stiff aluminium foil which is long enough to encircle a saucer. Silver is the colour most commonly available, but it can sometimes be obtained in gold or other colours. Make sure that the foil is fireproof.

First draw your design in pencil on tracing-paper. Secure this to the sheet of foil with sticky tape and place both on a thick pad of newspaper. This will enable the point to puncture the material easily, as well as protect your working surface. Pierce through the dots, varying the size of the holes by using different tools such as knitting needles, compass points, skewers, etc. Join together the two ends of the sheet with sticky tape to form a cylinder. Set a thick candle on a saucer and over this, stand the shade. The ideal position for the candle-flame is half-way up the shade.

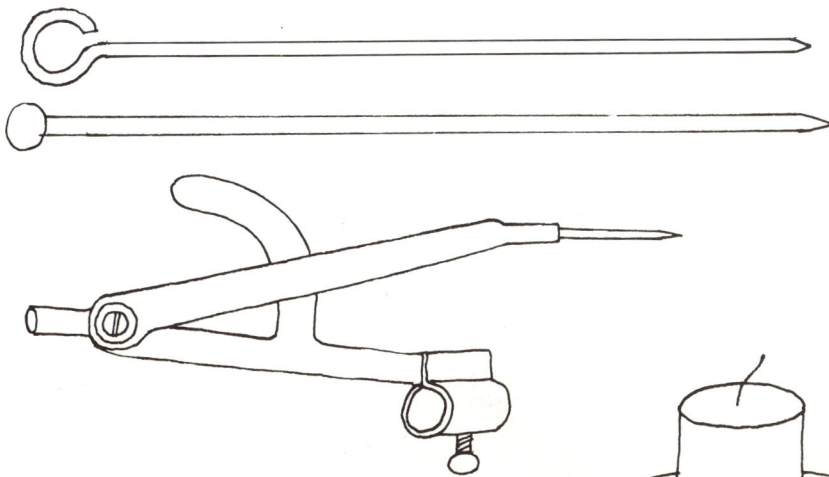

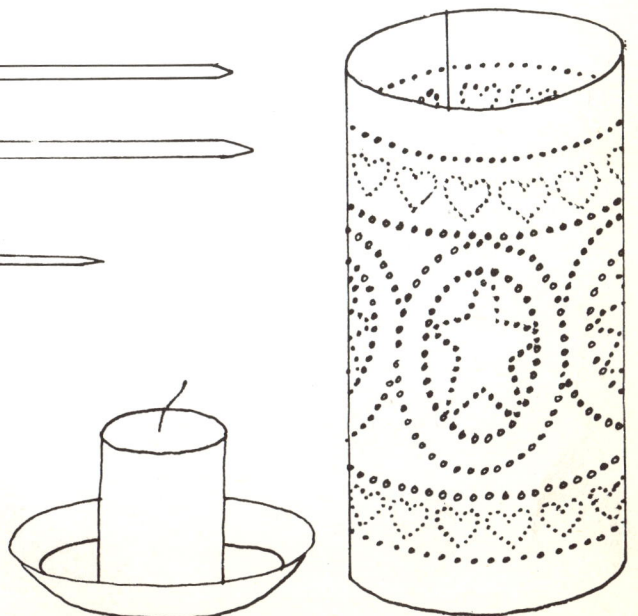

Egg Candle and Frills

For both designs above and those on the opposite page use fireproof foil. Cut a piece of foil 1 cm longer than the circumference of the candle or egg. Mark the design on the foil lightly with a sharp metal point before cutting out. Use sticky tape or glue to join the ends into a ring (see below).

Use pinking shears when cutting out the design at the bottom of this page.

The egg-holder design is intended to be a decoration for hard-boiled or blown eggs. It is too flimsy to use as a practical egg-cup.

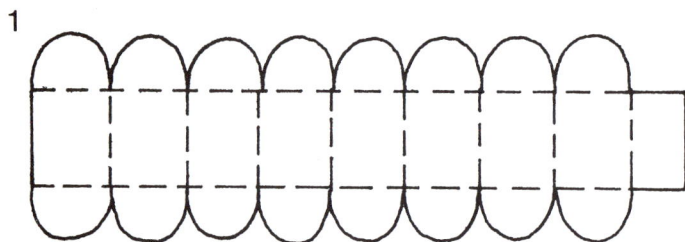

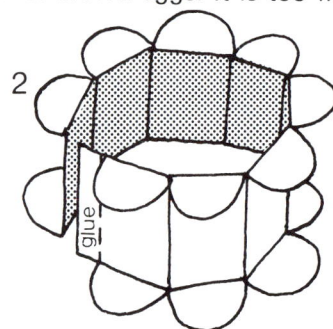

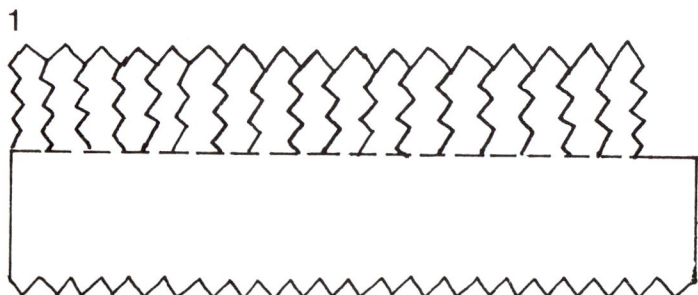

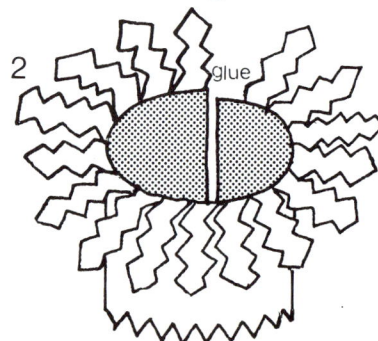

1

2

glue

1

2

glue

1

cut

1

fold

fold

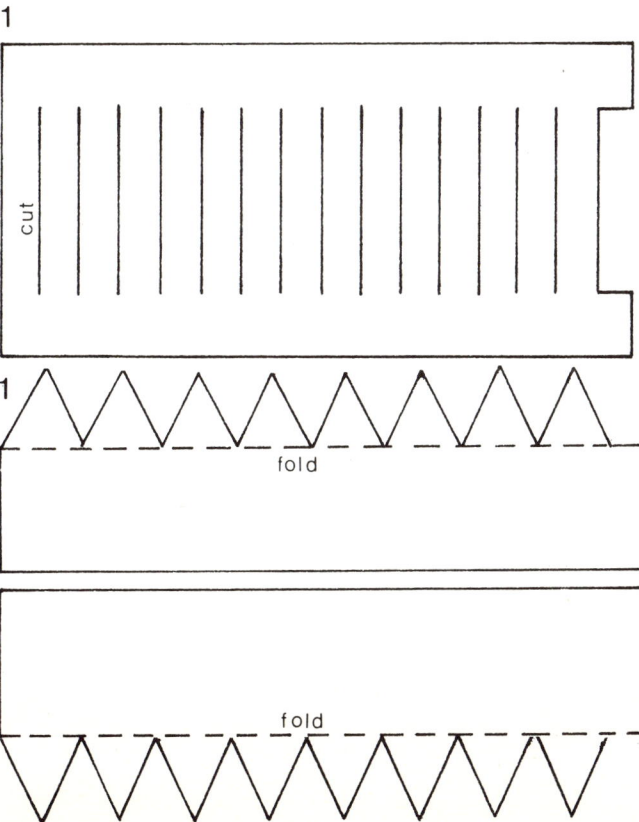

2

glue

3

glue
tab

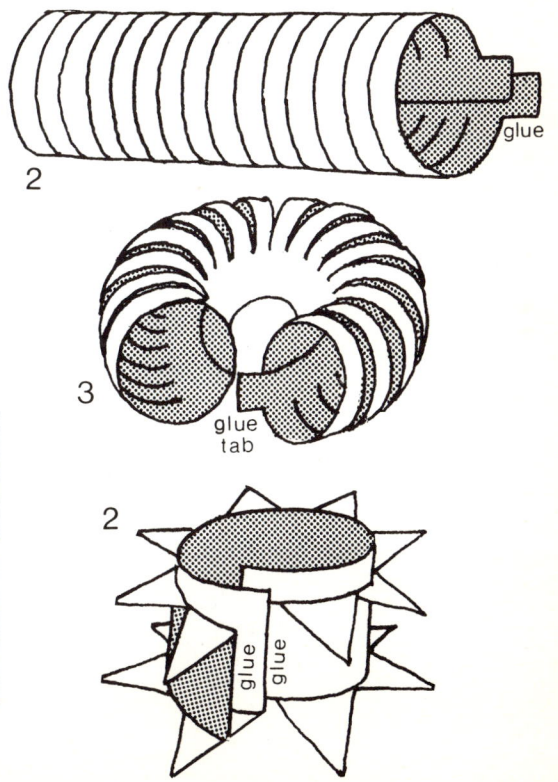

2

glue glue

Decorated Eggs

This method is known as 'batik' and is commonly used in Eastern Europe. You will need a jar lid, wire, a candle, an ounce of beeswax (can be bought from a chemist's shop), paraffin, feathers, food dye and blown eggs. (To blow an egg, make a small hole in each end. Hold the egg over a basin, blow firmly through one end until the egg is empty.) Cut the tips of the feathers into various shapes (1). Make a wire frame to hold the jar lid over the candle (2). Melt the beeswax in the lid and add an equal amount of paraffin to it. Heat the mixture over the candle but do not boil. Dip a feather in the liquid and press it lightly against an egg (3), on to which you have already drawn a pattern faintly with pencil (4). Your pattern can of course be a combination of the different feather shapes. Dip the egg into a bowl of food dye (5), then drain and dry it. When dry, hold the egg beside the candle-flame (not *over* the flame – the egg will turn black) to melt the wax. Wipe with a clean, soft cloth. Finally, polish the egg with a spot of olive oil and rub it with a dry cloth. Place the eggs in a basket or hang them from threads.

To help you plan your patterns, at the bottom of the page are examples of traditional ways of dividing eggs into sections before decorating them (6).

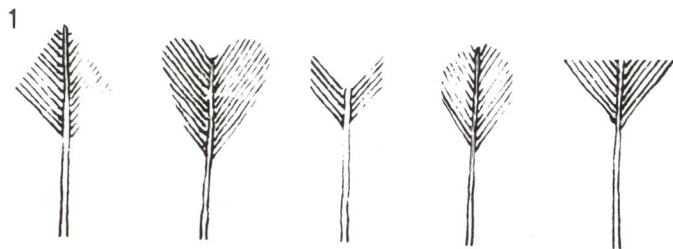

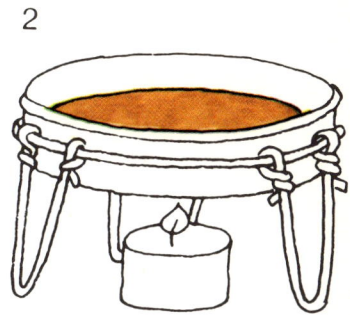

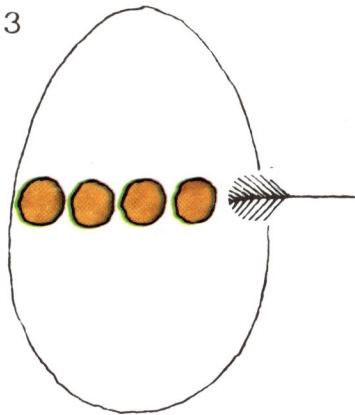

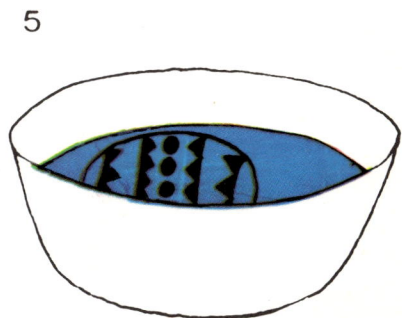

Christmas Fairy

Materials: thin white card, 1 white paper napkin, 1 ping-pong ball, silver card, silver foil, black tissue-paper, pipe cleaners, one drinking straw, elastic, cotton and a small piece of tinsel. For the main body, cut out a rectangle of thin card (1), bend it round and glue together to make a tube (2). At one end cut two V-shaped notches into which the arms will hook (3). Cut out the bodice shape, with a hole in the centre and with a slot from the hole to one end (4). Bend the bodice over the top of the roll (5) and secure each end with glue (6). For the head, take a ping-pong ball (7) and stick to it a neck of rolled, stiff paper (8). On the ball paint a face and hair. Make a top-knot from a small roll of fringed black tissue-paper (9 and 10). Stick it on and decorate with a silver-paper star (11). Make two arms from pieces of pipe cleaner (12). Cut out sleeves from a white paper napkin and tie them to the pipe cleaner with cotton (13). Turn the sleeves inside out (14) and tie the other end (15). Bend over the end of the pipe cleaner and glue each arm into its notch in the body (18). Make the skirt from a double thickness of paper napkin folded over a piece of elastic (16). Tie the ends of the elastic, gathering the skirt, and pull it up round the body of the fairy (17). Decorate the bodice and skirt with tinsel or strips of silver foil cut with pinking shears. Glue wings cut from silver card (19) on to the back of the doll and finally add a wand made from a drinking straw and tinsel (20).

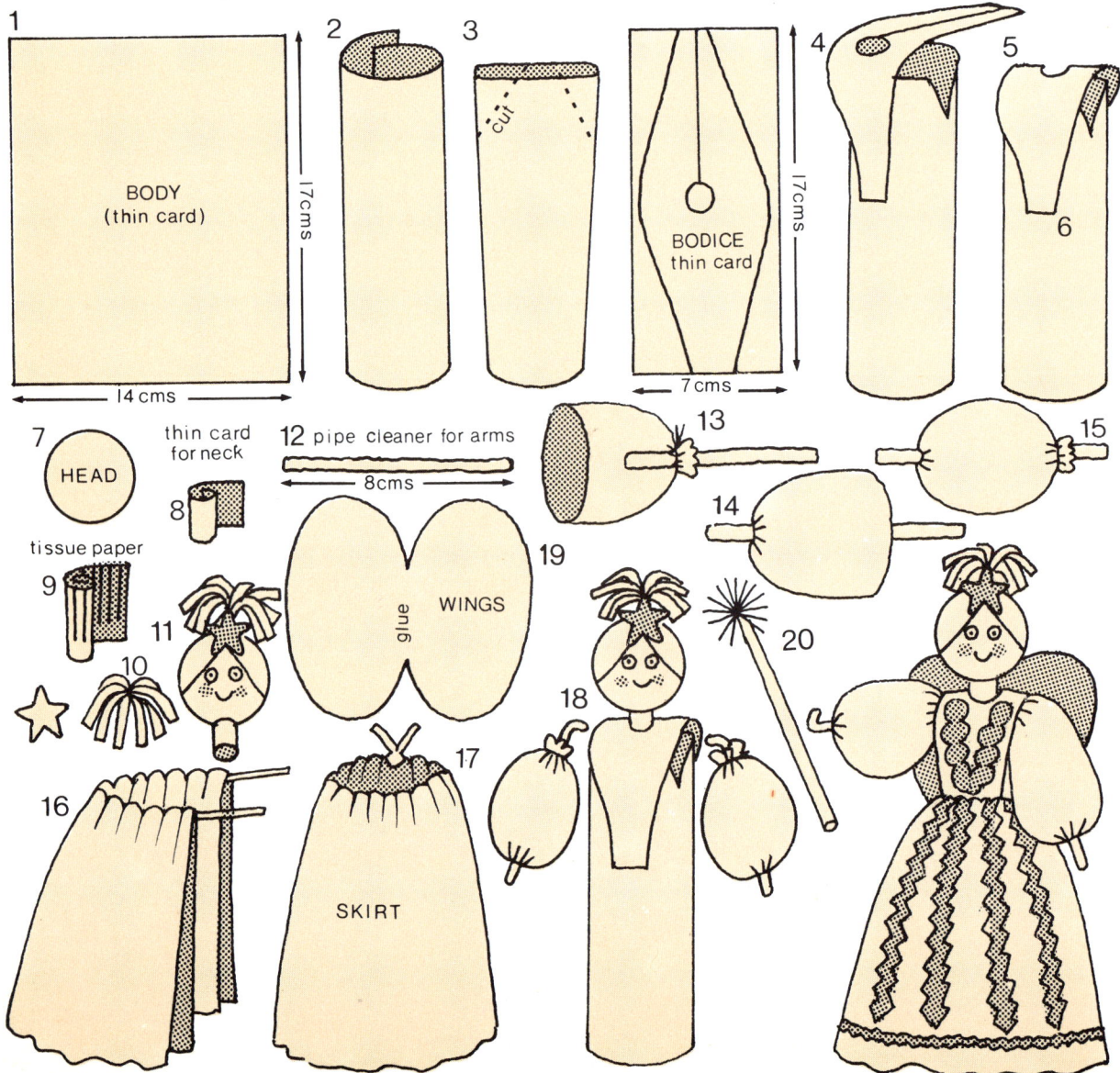

Miniature Christmas Tree

Place a stick into a lump of plasticine at the bottom of a paper cup. Make the main shape from paper folded into a cone and place this over the stick. Screw up squares of green tissue-paper and stick them on to the cone. Decorate the tree with small silver balls.

25cms

37cms

7cms

What Shall we Play?

A check-list of some of the games that have proved to be popular and most easily staged

Team Games

Nose Box Relay

Two teams stand in line one behind the other. Each team is given the outer case of a matchbox. This is placed on the nose of the first in line and is passed from nose to nose down the line without hands being used. The team that gets its matchbox to the end of the line first wins the race. If at any point the box is dropped, it must be returned to the front of the line and the passing starts all over again.

Chin the Orange

Two teams stand in line as for the previous game. This time the object to be passed down the line is an orange held by each player under his chin and transferred to beneath the chin of the next player, again without using hands. If at any point the orange is dropped, it must be returned to the front of the line to start its journey again.

Straw-sucking Relay

In this team-game a ball of tissue-paper is passed down the line. Each player transfers the tissue ball holding it by suction at the end of a drinking straw. If the paper is dropped, the passing must recommence at the front of the line.

Garter Race

Use a loop of elastic which is only just big enough when stretched to pass over the body of each player. The first player pulls it down over his head and shoulders and down over his feet and then passes it to his team-mate who repeats the process.

Water Race

This is a team-game that is definitely an *outdoor* game. Each team stands in a line, at the head of which is an empty bucket and some distance away a full bucket of water. The first member of each team has a tin or plastic mug and with this the team must transfer water from the full bucket to the empty one by running in turn up to the full bucket and bringing back a mug of water. When an agreed time limit has expired the amount of water collected by each team is measured (the buckets can be weighed on ordinary bathroom scales) and the team who has transferred the most water wins.

Every-man-for-himself Games

Kipper Race

Supply each player with a fish shape (about a foot long) cut from newspaper (obviously a batch of fishes can be cut together). Each player is also given a folded newspaper. On the word 'Go' each player blows his kipper along by whacking the floor just behind it with the folded newspaper. The first player to get a kipper over the line wins.

Bun-eating Race

A string is tied across the room. From this is hung short lengths of string — one for each player — on each of which is knotted (like a conker) a currant bun. The height of each bun must be adjusted so that the player has to stand on tiptoe to reach it with his mouth only (hands must not be used). The first one to finish eating the whole bun wins.

Spin the Plate

The players sit in a ring. One player goes to the centre of the ring and spins on the ground a metal or plastic plate on its edge. At the same time he calls out the name of one of the other players who must then run and grab the plate before it stops spinning and falls flat. If he manages to do so then it is his turn to spin the plate and to call out the name of another player; if he fails, he must pay a forfeit.

Balloon Games

Throw the Balloon

A line is made on the floor (with chalk, string or tape, or just use the edge of the carpet as a boundary line). Each player stands behind the line and throws a balloon in turn as far as possible. The landing-place of each balloon is noted and marked with a card bearing the player's name. The one that goes the farthest wins.

Whizzing Balloons

Standing behind a line, each player blows up a balloon of a different colour or one marked with the player's name. The balloon is held at the neck to keep it inflated until the word 'Go' when they are all released and whizz forward propelled by the escaping air. The balloon travelling the farthest wins.

Musical Games

For all these games it is important that the person stopping and starting the music should be hidden from the players.

Musical Chairs

Two rows of chairs are placed back to back, or alternately one facing one way and the next the other, one chair per player. The players march round the group of chairs in the same direction, in time to the music. When the music stops everyone must sit down but one chair has been removed. The person without a seat drops out. In this way the game continues until only two players are left competing for one chair and a final sit-down decides the winner.

layer of wrapping, leaving the winner holding the prize.

Musical Bumps

A more basic variation of the previous game. The players dance around until the music stops and then they all sit down quickly on the floor. The last person to be seated drops out. The music and dancing then continue along with the process of elimination until only the winner is left.

Pass the Parcel

The players sit in a ring. A prize wrapped in several layers of paper is passed round as the music plays. When it stops the player holding the parcel unwraps one layer. Then the music and the passing continue. Eventually the music stops for the last

Hot Potato

A sort of 'Pass the Parcel' in reverse. A smooth object such as a plastic ball is passed round as the music plays, and the player left holding the object when the music stops has to drop out. This means that each player passes on the object with a sense of panic.

Musical Hats

Similar to 'Hot Potato' but each player must put on, take off and pass along a hat, making sure he's not left holding or wearing it when the music stops. Don't attempt to use a paper hat — it's unlikely to last more than a couple of rounds.

Blindfold Games

Blind Man's Buff

One player is blindfolded, spun round three times and left to catch one of the other players. If he succeeds he must guess — by feeling the face — whom he has caught. If he guesses correctly that person takes over as Blind Man.

Tail on the Donkey

Draw the outline of a donkey (minus tail) on a large sheet of paper. Draw and cut out separately the donkey's tail and tape a drawing pin on to it. If possible fix the donkey drawing to a surface into which one can easily stick a pin or, failing that, use adhesive tape to attach the tail. Each player in turn is blindfolded and attempts to put the donkey's tail in the appropriate place. The position of each attempt is marked with the player's name

and the player who gets nearest to the target wins.

Thief, Thief!

A blindfolded player is seated on the floor and must guard his 'treasure' (a collection of assorted small objects) placed in front of him. The other players must stand behind a line at a distance of say 15 feet. From there they must sneak up and try to steal an object from him (only one object at a time) and take that object back behind their line. The keeper of the treasure is armed with a rolled-up newspaper. When he thinks a thief is near he shouts 'Thief, Thief!' and hits out. Any thief hit by the newspaper must go back to the line and start again. A time is recommended for the keeper — or until he has caught, say, four players.

Search Games

Collecting

Give each player or pair of players a different list of assorted objects for which they must search all over the house. To avoid the ransacking of drawers and cupboards arrange each object (such as a thimble, a shoebrush, a clothes-peg, etc.) in fairly accessible places. For a summer party the list of objects could include such things as a sycamore seed, a smooth pebble, a feather, etc. The first to complete their list wins.

Treasure Hunt

For children of about seven years or more, who can easily read simply written clues, quite complicated games can be devised depending on the time available for preparation beforehand.

Each player (or each pair of players) is given a clue on a piece of paper giving directions to the location of the next clue and so on until the last clue gives the actual location of the 'treasure' itself. The ingenuity of the children can be tested by writing the clues in the form of riddles or in lettering that can only be read when reflected in a mirror, or the clue can be torn into several pieces which must be assembled in order to be read.

Quiet Games

Silent Champion

The players lie face down on the floor and must remain completely still. Any player who moves a muscle or makes a sound (according to the judgement of a referee) must drop out of the game. By this process of elimination the player capable of remaining silent and immobile for the longest time is champion.

Kim's Game

Make a selection of about fifteen to twenty common objects such as a safety pin, a spoon, a cotton reel, a button, etc. Place them on a tray and cover them with a cloth. The players gather round, the cloth is removed for say two minutes and then the players (who have each been given pencil and paper) have to write down as many objects as they can remember. The player who makes the longest correct list within a set time limit is the winner.

Keep-it-to-yourself

All players leave the room except one who places a small object (previously agreed on by everyone) in a place where it can be seen but only after some fairly hard scrutiny. For instance it could be placed amongst some books on a shelf, on the frame of a doorway or under a chair. The other players return to the room and look for the object. Any player finding it must not touch it or say anything but simply sit down. When everyone has made the discovery, the player who first did so can then hide the next object.

Food Glorious Food

Have as much fun preparing the food
as your friends will have devouring it

Bread

White Bread (below)
1½ lbs plain white flour
1 level teaspoon salt
½ oz lard
½ oz fresh baker's yeast
and 1 level teaspoon caster sugar
¾ pint warm water

Wholemeal Bread (opposite)
1½ lbs plain wholemeal flour
1 level teaspoon salt
½ oz lard
1 oz fresh baker's yeast
and 1 level teaspoon caster sugar
¾ pint warm water

Method for both white and wholemeal: Sift the flour and salt and rub in the lard. Add warm water to the yeast and sugar, then mix this liquid with dry ingredients. Work into a firm dough until the sides of the bowl are clean. Turn the dough on to a floured surface and knead well. Leave in a warm place in a greased, covered bowl until it has doubled its size (about an hour). Turn the risen dough on to a floured surface and knead again. Now you are ready to make something.

Bread Mat   Make long 'snakes' of dough and arrange on a greased baking-tray. Brush the whole with beaten egg and sprinkle with poppy seeds. Leave to rise for 30 minutes and bake in a hot oven 450 °F (Mark 8) for 15–20 minutes.

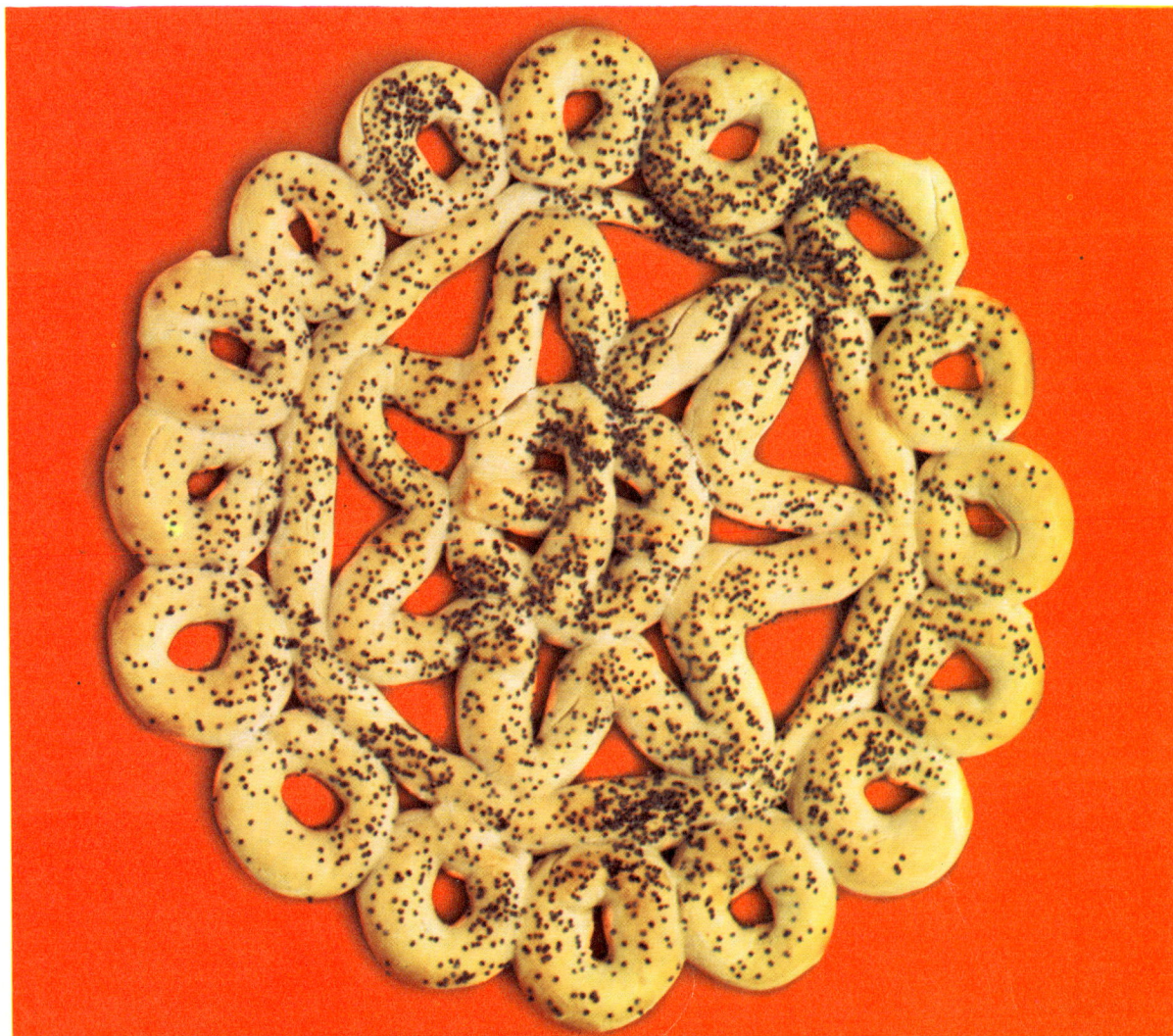

Bread Figures   Use dough as you would plasticine, and arrange the figures on a baking-tray. (If the joins don't stick, moisten them gently with beaten egg.) Leave to rise for 30 minutes and bake them for the same time and at the same temperature as the bread mat. On page 94 there is a bread alphabet.

Sandwiches

Among the left-overs of a party you will usually find a fair proportion of sad-looking sandwiches. Why not make them more attractive and then perhaps they'll stand a chance against the cakes and jellies? Use pastry-cutters to make the main shapes. Cut the eye-holes for the faces with icing nozzles. Use a dark filling (say fish paste) so that through the holes it shows up against the white bread. The other variation shown on the plate below is made from one thickness of bread, plus its filling, rolled up into a miniature swiss-roll.

Opposite: A mosaic of sandwich squares and triangles.

Biscuits

10 oz plain flour
½ teaspoon salt
6 oz butter
7 oz pale, soft brown sugar
1 large beaten egg
2 oz cooking chocolate
Currants for eyes

The above quantities make four ladies the size of the drawing at the bottom of the page, or one lady this size and a selection of the faces shown on the next two pages.

Method: Sift the flour and salt. Cream the sugar and butter until pale and light textured. Add the beaten egg. Add the dry ingredients to make a creamy mixture. Melt the chocolate in a small bowl over a saucepan of hot water. Divide the dough into three parts and mix one part with the melted chocolate. Put this dark, sticky mixture in the fridge for about 15 minutes to harden. Colour the second part of the dough pink by using red food dye. Leave the third part in its original colour. You now have three different-coloured balls of biscuit mixture to model with. Roll them out until they are about ½ cm thick. In each case cut out the main body shapes on the greased baking-tray rather than attempt to transfer them later. The smaller shapes, such as eyes, hats, hair, etc., can be cut out on another surface and added. Press patterns into the dough with different kinds of icing nozzles. Bake at 350 °F (Mark 4) for 8—10 minutes.

Opposite is my own biscuit lady and on the following two pages are examples of the great variety of biscuit people you can make. There are two more complete biscuit figures on the front and back of the book.

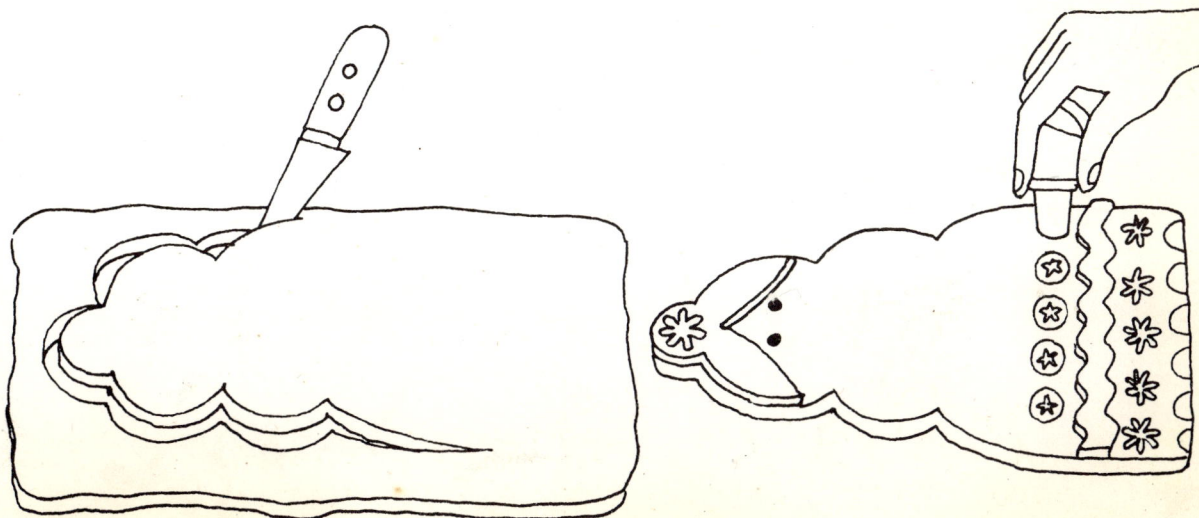

Sugar Babies

1 lb icing sugar
1 large egg-white
1 full tablespoon of glucose liquid (obtainable from a chemist)
Cornflour for flouring board
Food dyes

The above quantities make about two dozen babies, 5 cm long. Alternatively some of the mixture could be used for the mice, bunnies and chicks shown over the page.

Sieve the icing sugar. Place the egg-white and glucose in a bowl. Add icing sugar and stir with a wooden spoon until the mixture binds together. Knead with finger-tips until it becomes pliable and smooth. Break off a sixth of the mixture and into it mix three drops of red food dye. This is for the pink faces. Take a sixth of this lump and add another two drops of red to make a stronger pink for the babies' cheeks.

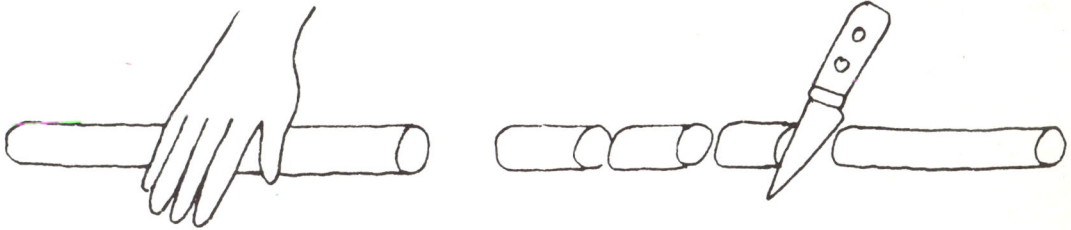

Sprinkle your board with cornflour and roll out the main white lump into a 'snake' about 2 cm thick.

Cut this into pieces 5 cm long and round off the ends to make the main baby-shape.

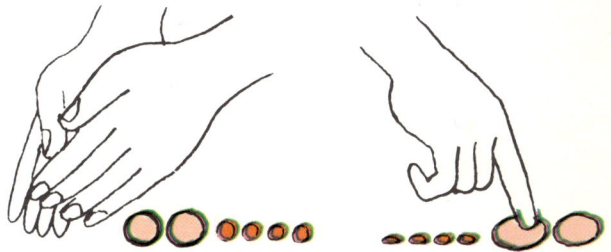

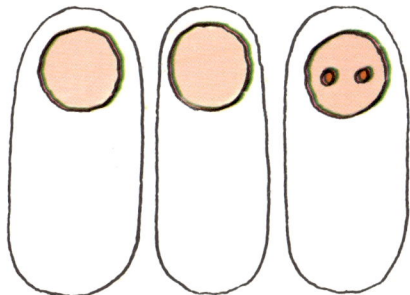

To make the faces, roll small balls, press flat and place them on the bodies. Make smaller balls from 'cheeks' mixture and press them on flat.

Decorate the babies with a mixture of icing sugar and egg-white (see page 71 for a piping recipe).

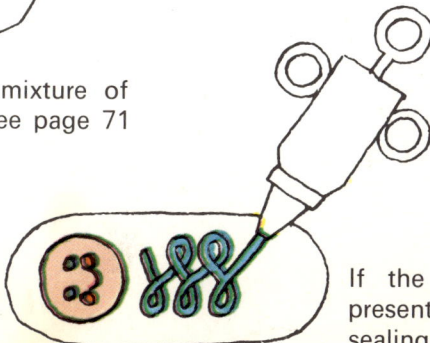

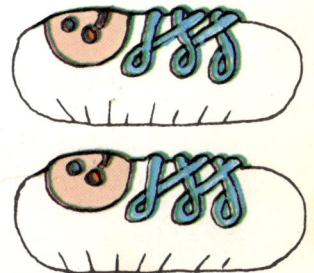

If the babies are to be 'take-home' presents they can be covered with self-sealing transparent wraps.

Sugar Bunnies *(These quantities make eight rabbits 7 cm high)*

Make the main shape from the same mixture as the babies. Make a ball for the body, a smaller one for the head and four even smaller ones for the legs. Make ear-shapes from the pink-coloured mixture and dent them with a knife. Assemble the parts and press in silver-ball eyes and nose. When dry, tie a real ribbon round the bunny's neck.

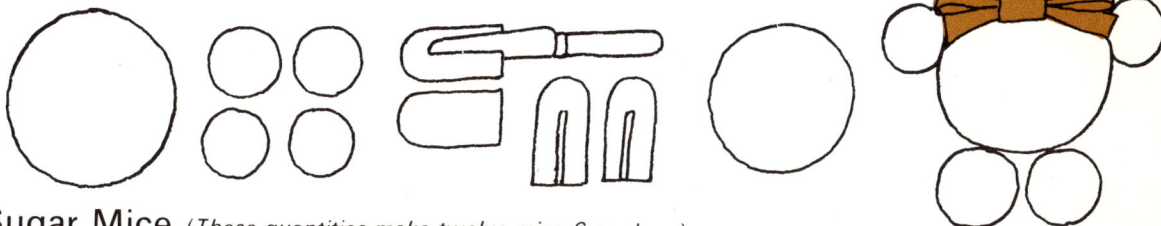

Sugar Mice *(These quantities make twelve mice 6 cm long)*

Make the main shape from the same mixture as the bunnies. From a packet of flaked almonds choose good shapes for ears, and use silver balls for the eyes. Poke in a piece of string as a tail and thread some white cotton through the nose, trimming it to make whiskers.

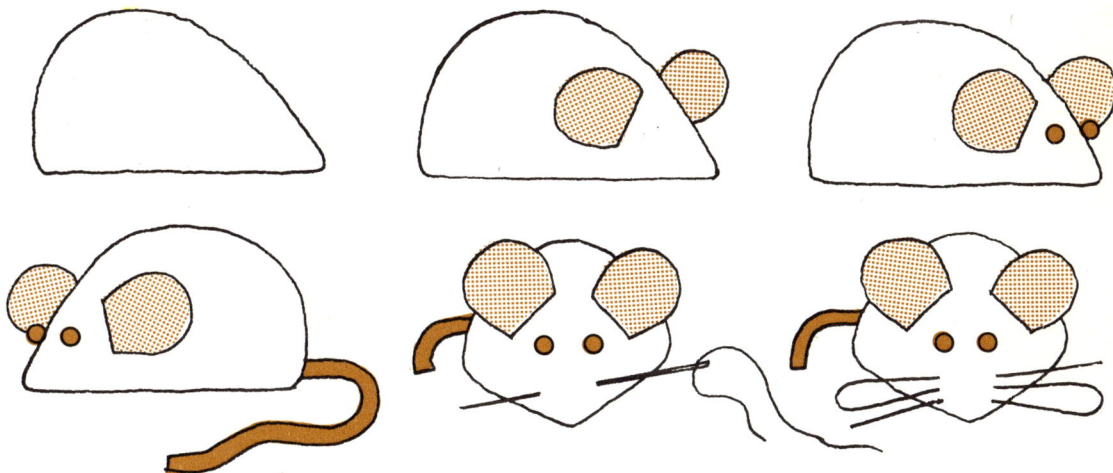

Sugar Chicks *(These quantities make ten chicks)*

This time colour all the mixture yellow and break off enough for the beaks. By adding just a few drops of red to this smaller part you will have a lovely orange. From the main lump make a ball for the body and cut at the sides for the wings. Add a smaller ball for the head. Roll out the orange mixture and cut out diamond shapes for beaks. Fold them over and join them on to the head, adding silver balls for eyes.

A chick could sit at each place on the table holding a name-card in its beak.

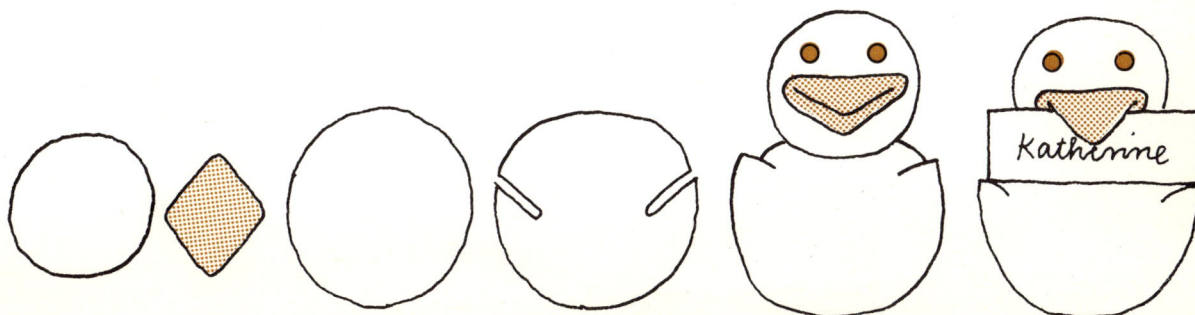

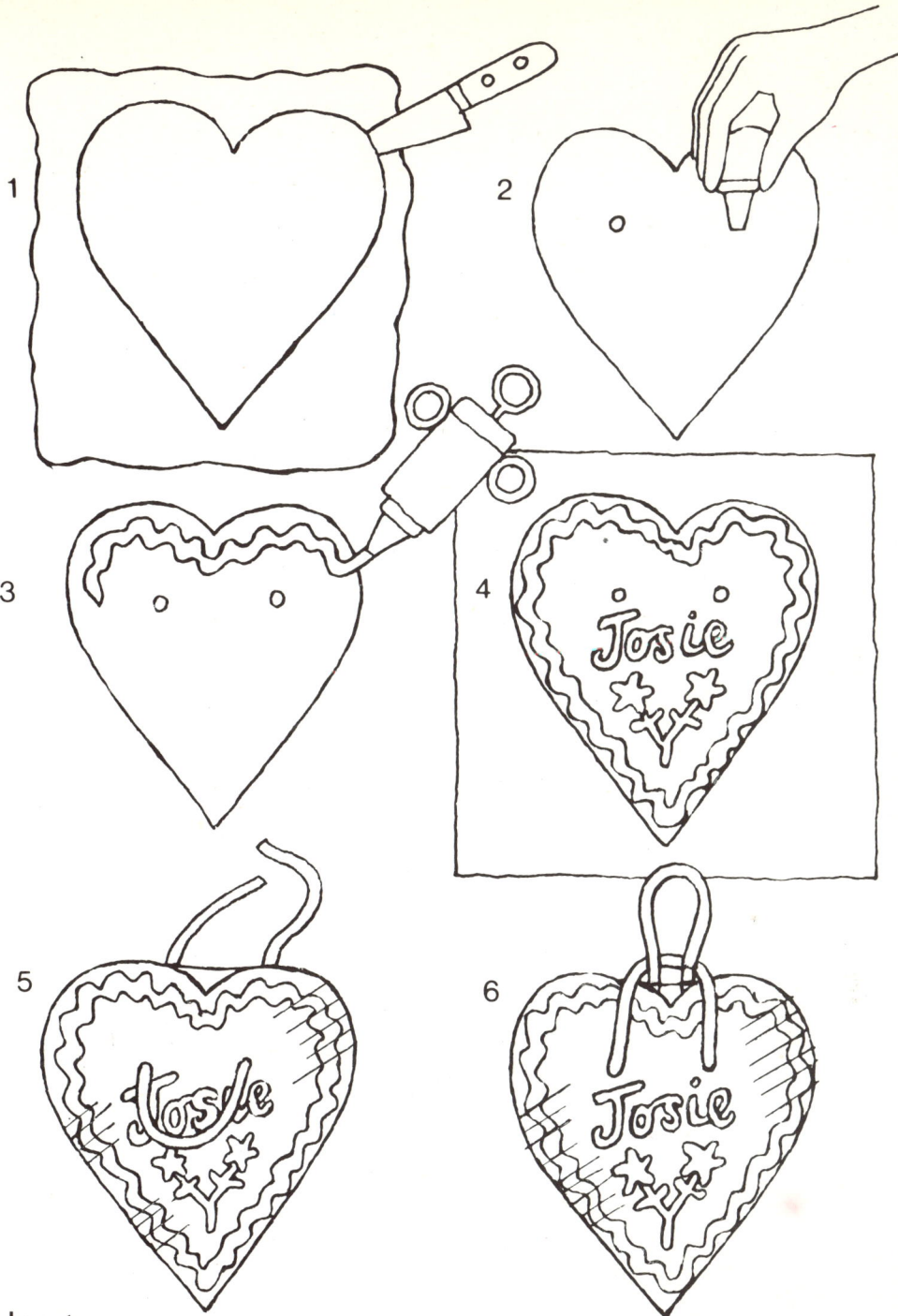

Biscuit Hearts

Make the biscuit mixture given on page 63 but add 2 oz more chocolate to the ingredients.

When you have rolled out the dough, place on a greased baking-tray (1) and cut out the heart with a knife (2). Press out holes for ribbon with an icing nozzle. Bake at 350°F (Mark 4) for 8–10 minutes. Allow to cool. Decorate the heart with piping icing. This is made by beating one egg-white until frothy and gradually adding sieved icing sugar until the mixture is stiff enough for piping (3). For the different colours divide the icing into separate cups and add drops of the appropriate food dye.

If it is to be a going-home present, wrap the heart in self-sealing transparent film, joining it at the back (4). Thread a ribbon through the holes and tie it at the back. Pass the ribbon through itself to make a loop (5).

Meringue Characters

Excellent meringues can be made from packaged 'instant' meringue mixes, but if you wish to make your own, here is a basic method.

Add a pinch of salt to three egg-whites and whisk them until stiff. (If the bowl can be turned upside down and the mixture stays put, it's stiff enough.) Gradually fold in 6 oz caster sugar with a metal spoon.

Pipe the mixture, using a nozzle with a large round hole, on to a greased flat baking-tray. Bake in the bottom of a cool oven at 200 °F (Mark $\frac{1}{2}$ or $\frac{1}{4}$) for 3–4 hours until the meringues are dried out but not long enough to turn them brown.

Slide meringues off tray with a large, flat knife.

Decorate the meringues with chocolate icing. Mix together 6 oz icing sugar, 2 oz melted plain chocolate and enough of one egg-white to make the mixture consistent for piping. Decorate quickly before the melted chocolate sets.

Sausage Safari

To make the alligator below, cut the cucumber at one end to form a mouth (1) and prop it open with sliced almond teeth (2). Insert four cocktail-stick 'legs' into the alligator's tummy to prevent the cucumber from rolling (3), disguising them with green cut-paper feet attached with sticky tape. Add sweets as eyes, stuck on with cocktail sticks (4). The main shape of the hedgehog (opposite) is a mound of mashed potato. The eyes can be made from crispy potato rings and the nose from the end of a sausage.

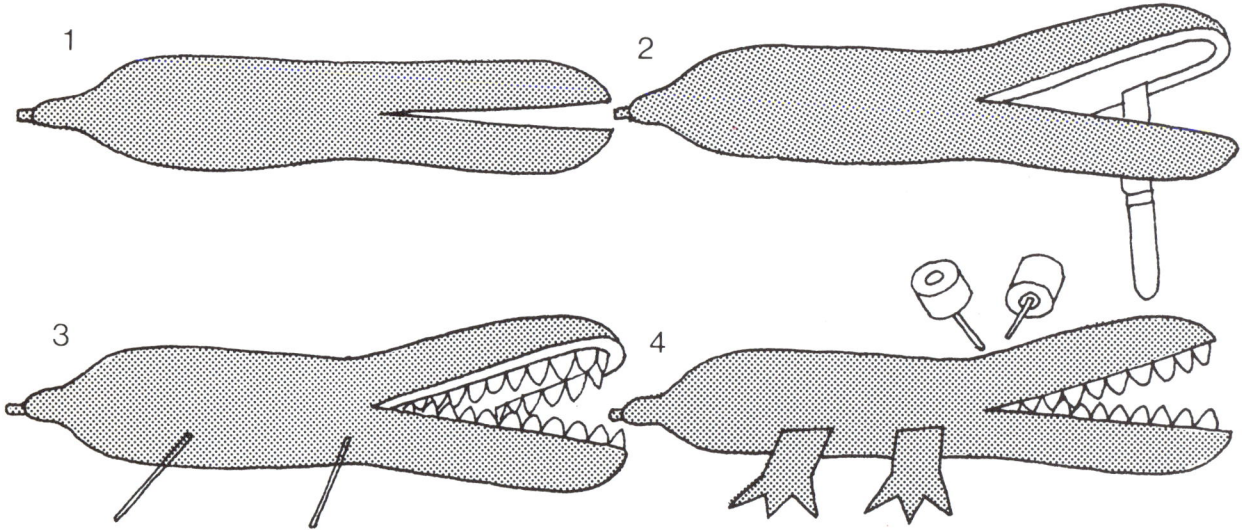

Crispy Collages

Savoury crisps and biscuits are now available in a great variety of shapes. A selection can be displayed on a tray or paper table-cloth as a kind of collage, like the dragon below or the sun-burst opposite.

Hansel-and-Gretel Cake

8 oz butter
8 oz caster sugar
4 eggs
8 oz self-raising flour
Juice and rind of ½ lemon

Method: Cream the butter and sugar until white and fluffy. Add the eggs one at a time each with a teaspoonful of boiling water. Fold in the sifted flour with a wooden spoon and finally add the lemon juice. Place the mixture in a 17 cm square cake tin. Arrange the mixture leaving a dip in the middle. This dip will compensate for the rising that would normally occur there and in this case, a flat-topped cake is required. Bake in the centre of the oven at 350 °F (Mark 4) for 1 hour. Most of the cakes on the following pages can also be made from this recipe.

Slice the cake into sections and from these build the house as shown in the diagram. Use the butter icing recipe (below) to join the pieces together. Put the various sweets in place before the butter icing sets.

Butter icing
8 oz butter
12 oz icing sugar
2–4 tablespoons milk
Cream the butter until soft. Gradually beat in sugar, adding the milk.

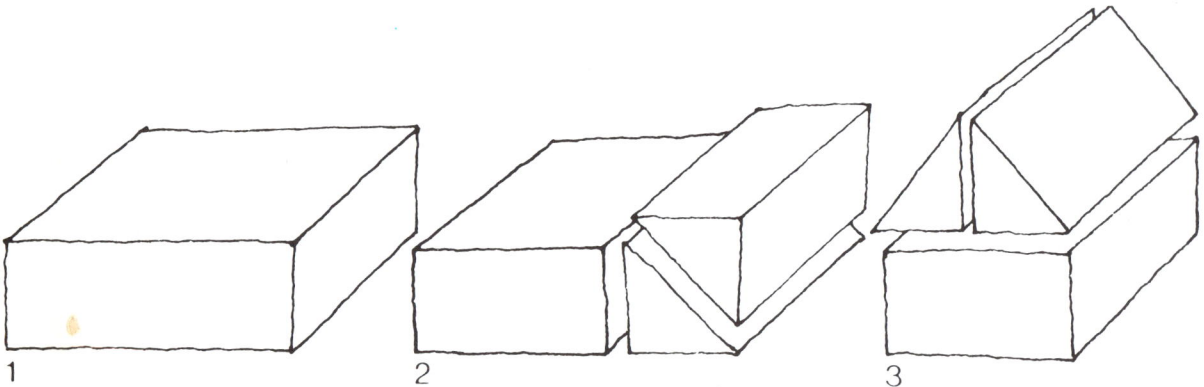

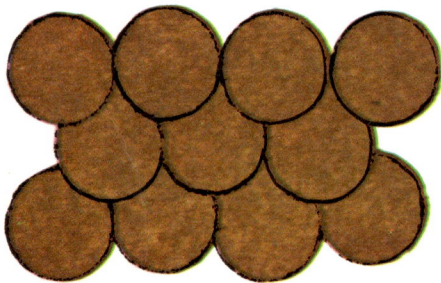

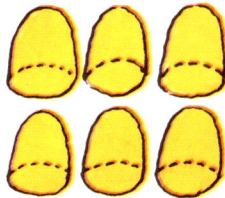

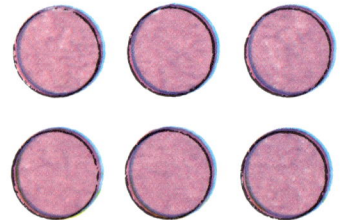

Chocolate Engine Cake

This chocolate engine can be made quickly from ready-made chocolate cakes and biscuits and a Walnut Whip. Stick the parts together with chocolate butter icing (the icing recipe on page 78, plus 2 oz of melted chocolate).

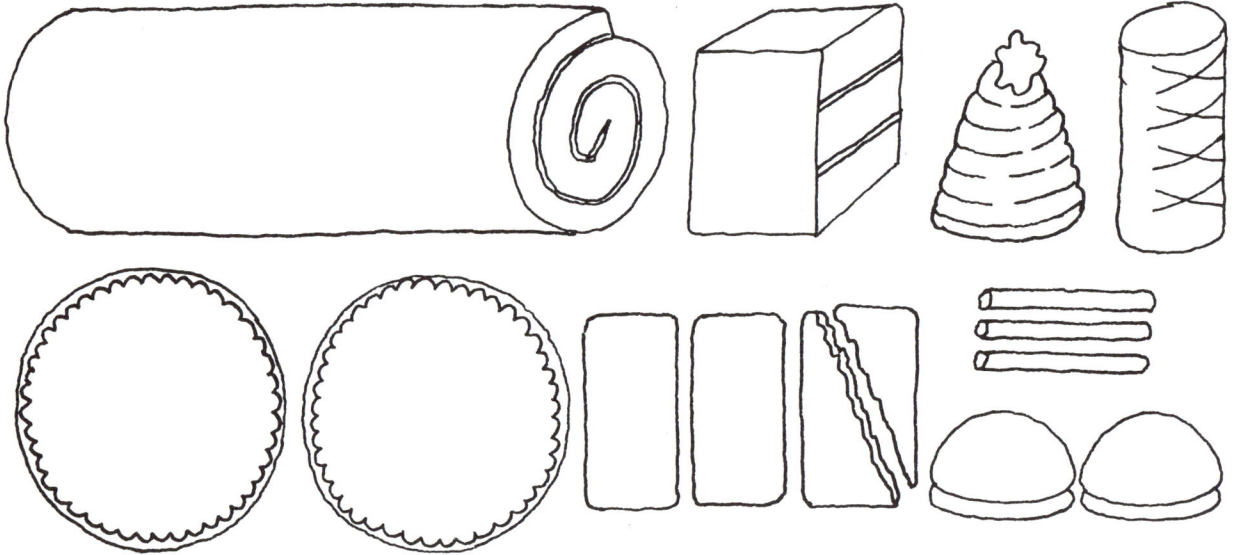

Ship Cake

Make this ship from a basic square cake (see page 78 for recipe). Add mini chocolate swiss rolls for funnels. Cover with butter icing (recipe page 78) and use piping icing for the final decoration (see page 71).

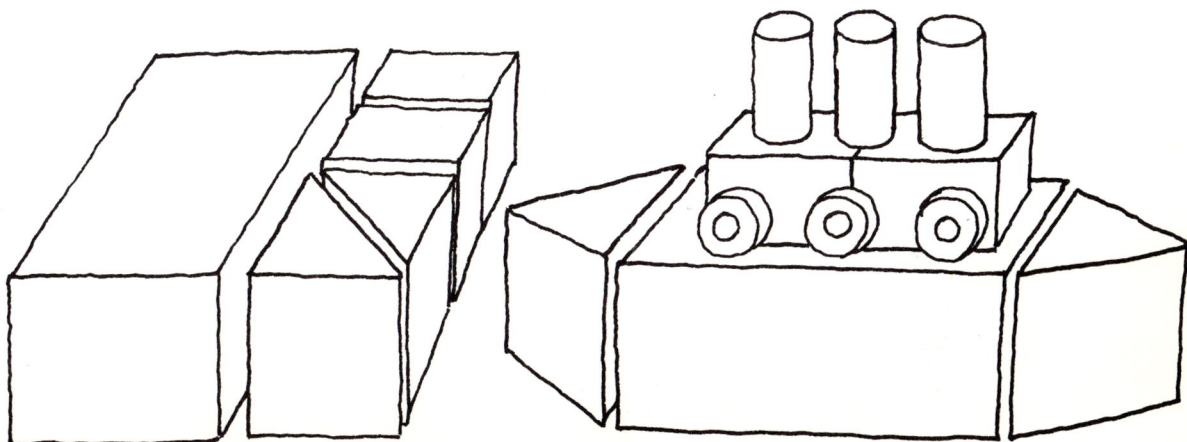

Fort and Bed Cakes

Fort David is also made from a basic square cake (see page 78 for recipe), plus a smaller block for the cabin, all covered in chocolate butter icing (see page 78 for recipe). The stockade is lined with chocolate sticks. The Bed cake opposite is made of three sections but economically from a square cake (see below), and decorated with both butter icing and piping icing. The recipe and method for making the bunnies' heads are on page 69.

The Party's Over

Give your friends a happy send-off with simple presents either made by you or bought and wrapped up in an exciting way

Necklaces

Straw Necklace

Cut coloured or striped drinking straws into short lengths of about 5 cm. Thread them together, with a wooden bead between each straw.

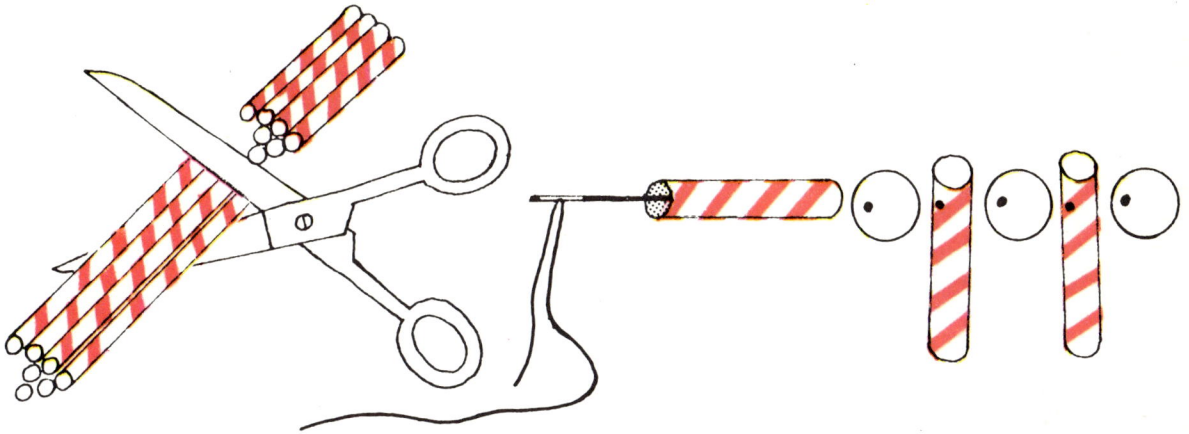

Paper Bead Necklace

Cut wedge-shaped strips of paper about 7 cm long by 3 cm at the widest end. Cut these from old, coloured glossy magazines. Starting with the wide end, roll each strip tightly round a knitting-needle. Glue the tip of the strip to prevent it unrolling and slide the knitting-needle out. Thread the paper beads together.

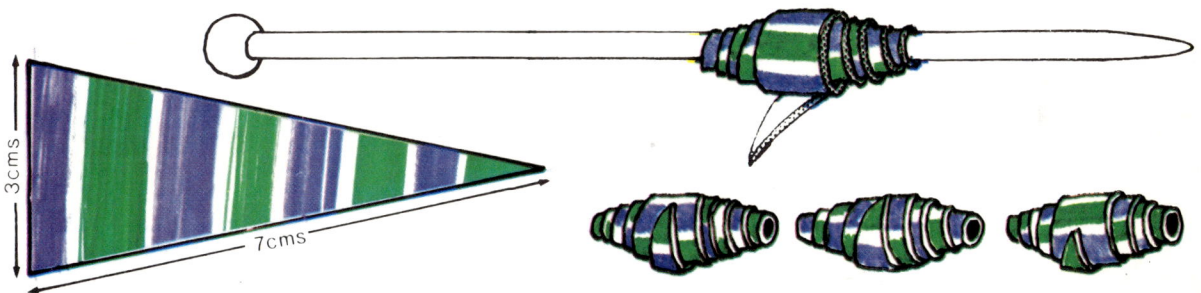

Crispy Ring Necklace

Thread potato crispy rings together on a brightly coloured or striped length of wool.

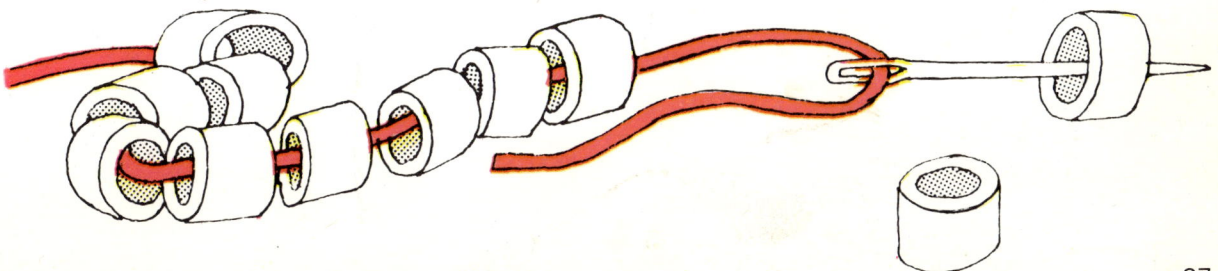

Dolls

Head: Wrap a marble in crêpe paper and make hair from untwisted coloured string (see diagram). Do not stick on the hair yet.

Arms: Roll paper tightly round a length of wire and tie in the middle. Make the puffed sleeves from looser rolls of paper; tie them, turn them in-side out towards the middle of the arm section and tie again. Glue the head to the centre of the arms.

Underskirt: Make a tight bunch of paper and tie it at the top.

Assembly: Make two straps of twice-folded paper. Stick the two ends to the back of the underskirt,

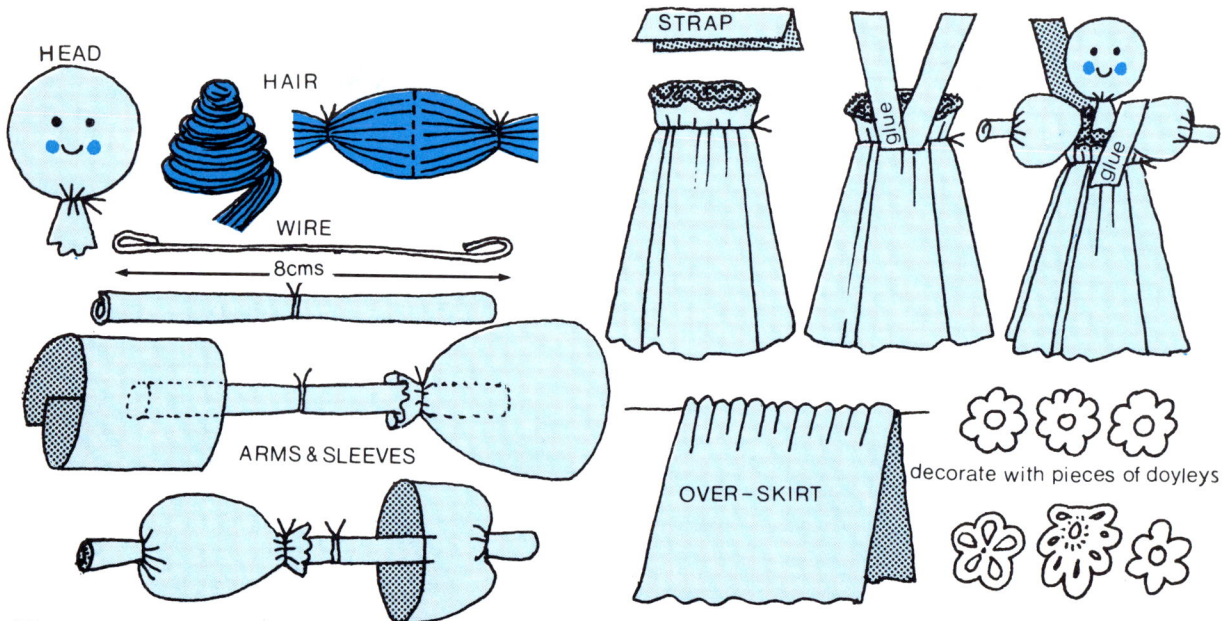

HEAD

HAIR

WIRE

8cms

ARMS & SLEEVES

STRAP

glue

glue

OVER-SKIRT

decorate with pieces of doyleys

Danish Sweetheart

fold over and stick the other ends to the front. This secures the head and arms section. Wrap the overskirt round and tie it tightly at the back with a cotton drawstring. Finally attach the hair with glue.

Note: The angel has a gown tied at her neck instead of an overskirt.

To make the Danish Sweetheart, cut two shapes of equal size from different coloured wrapping-paper. Fold them and cut a slot in each exactly the same length as the folded edge. Interlace them as shown below. You then have a little heart-shaped purse into which you can put sweets.

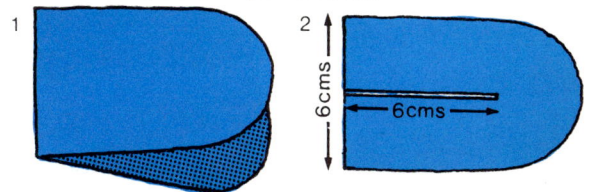

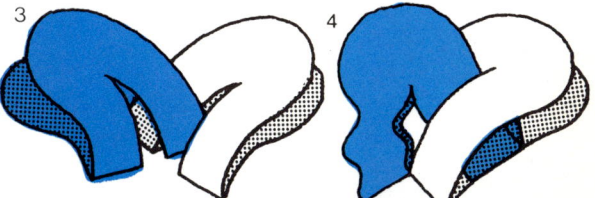

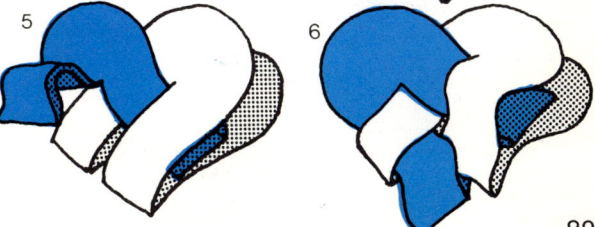

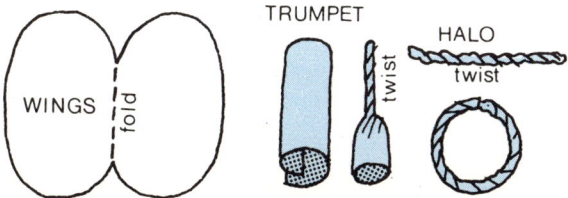

89

Wrapping-up *(See photographs on previous spread)*

Floppy Bird

To wrap up a long, thin present (such as three pencils or a pen) make a roll of tissue-paper about four times as long as the present. Insert the present so that one end of it is half-way along the roll, then flatten the roll on either side of the present. Shred it at one end to make the tail. Fold as shown and secure with sticky tape. Cut the face, wings and beak out of thin card. Assemble as shown.

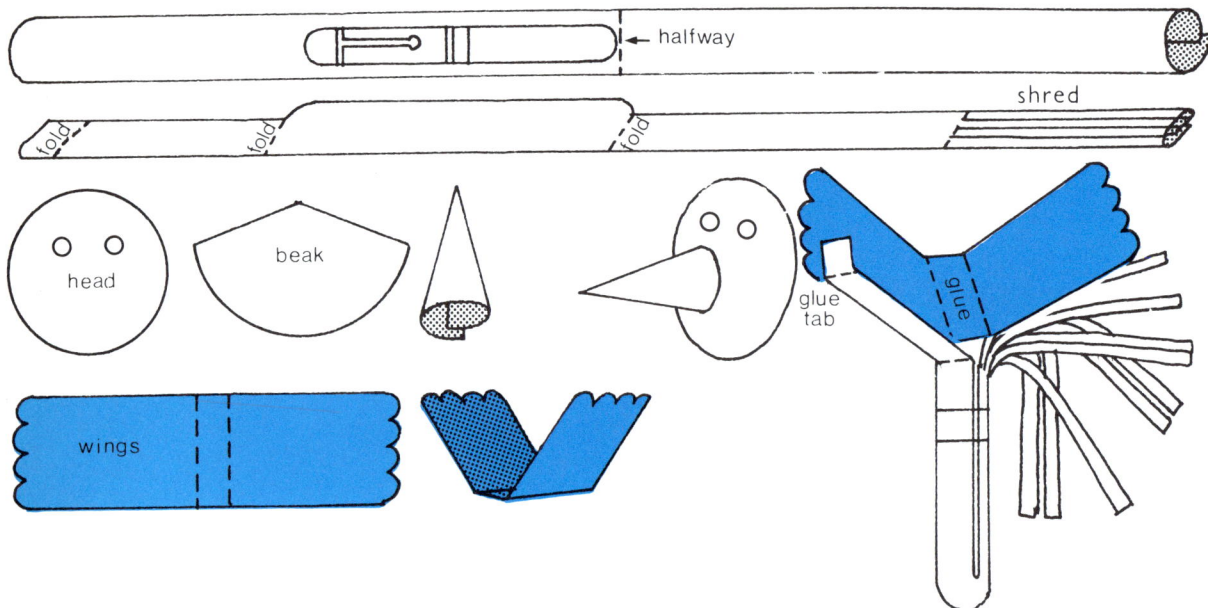

Boxbird

To package a small present (such as a ring or a toy soldier) cover the outer case of an empty matchbox with coloured paper. Insert the present in the matchbox drawer and cover the whole box with black tissue-paper. Stick on cut-paper eyes, beak, feet and wings with quick-drying glue.

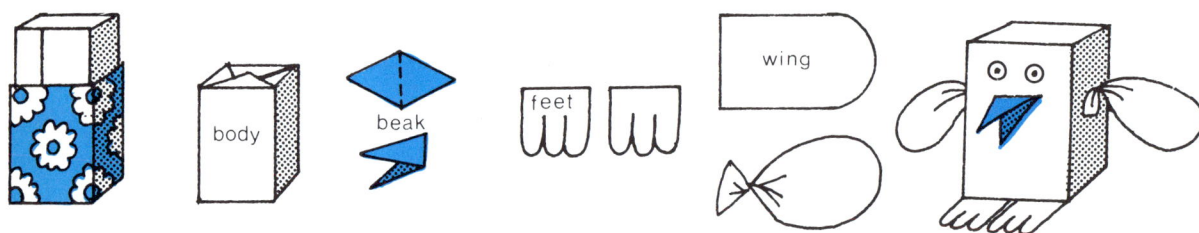

Daisy Head

Wrap up a long-shaped present in green tissue-paper and tie with coloured ribbon. Cut the leaves out of stiffer paper, draw the face on a paper cake-cup and glue them both in place.

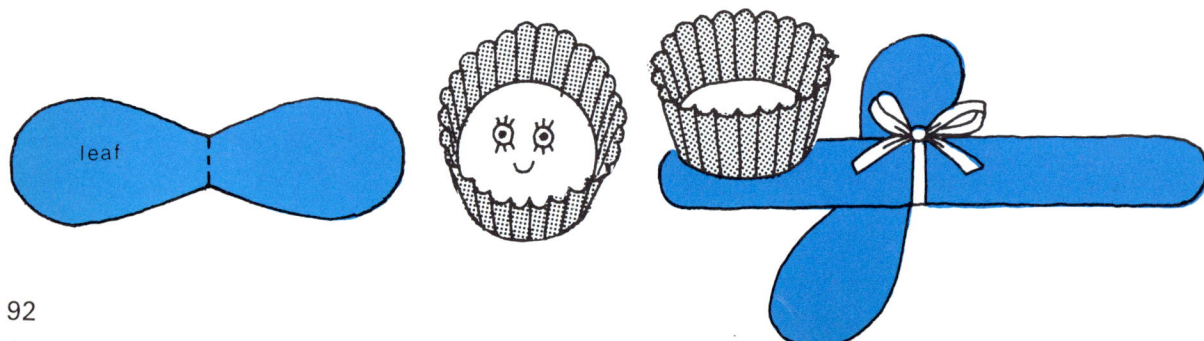

Dog Parcel

Wrap up a rectangular present (such as a miniature paintbox or a bar of chocolate) in striped or spotted paper. Stick some of the same paper on to thin card. Draw and cut out the face, ears and tail. Make holes for the brass clips and attach the ears. Glue the head and the tail to the body.

Cracker Parcel

Cut a rectangle from stiff paper three times the length of your present and draw guide lines (1). These will help you fold the paper as shown (2). Fold back the outer panels and cut notches (3). Unfold as shown below and decorate at ends and centre with brightly coloured paper. Make a cardboard tube or cut an empty toilet-roll to the length of your present. Roll the outer cover round the tube, and glue. Place the present inside the tube and tie the two 'necks' of the cracker with thread.

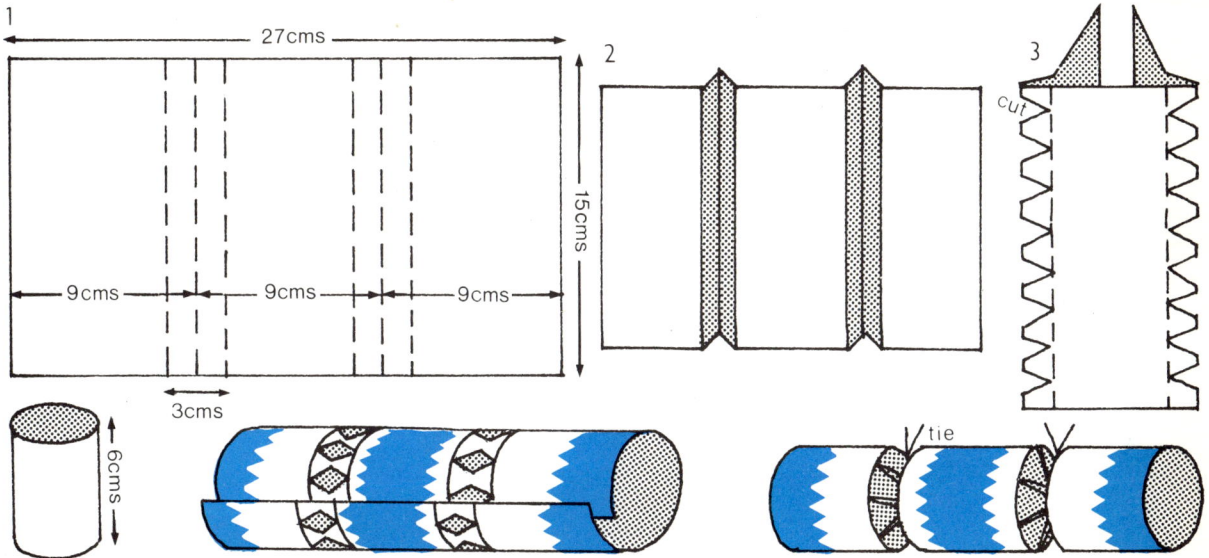

Label

Cut out a white heart, stick it on to coloured or metallic paper. Cut round the shape with pinking shears.

ABCDEF
GHIJKLM
NOPQRST
UVWXYZ

Index

Maureen Roffey

Maureen Roffey was trained at the Royal College of Art, and then worked for three years for Rediffusion Television, doing captions and illustrations. Since her marriage Maureen Roffey has worked freelance in book illustration, advertising, children's television, and designing and producing children's toys and cards. She has drawn two board books for the Bodley Head, *Indoors* and *Out-of-Doors*, and the first of her successful picture books, *Who killed Cock Robin?* was published in 1971, followed by *Farming with Numbers* in 1972 and *A Bookload of Animals* in 1973. Maureen Roffey is married to Bernard Lodge, a designer for BBC Television, and they have three children, David, Josephine and Katherine.